YOUR PASTOR, YOUR SHEPHERD

YOUR PASTOR, YOUR SHEPHERD

James Lee Beall

Edited by Marjorie Barber

LOGOS INTERNATIONAL
PLAINFIELD, NEW JERSEY

YOUR PASTOR, YOUR SHEPHERD

Printed in the United States of America

International Standard Book Number: 0-88270-216-5
Library of Congress Catalog Card Number: 77-77579
Publisher: Logos International
Plainfield, New Jersey 07061

To my son,
John Patrick Beall
The future should be exciting!

Table of Contents

FOREWORD
Spotlight on "Shepherds"

"Is the church relevant today, or are we living in a 'post-Christian era'? What is the role of the pastor or shepherd? How many sheep can be properly tended and fed in one flock?" These and many similar questions have become the topic of the day among church people. Particularly among charismatics the subject of shepherding the sheep has become an occasion for serious discussion and even controversy. Anyone who has kept abreast of the media knows that the spotlight has been turned upon shepherds.

Almost as pressing an issue among charismatics is the question of guidance. Many of these people spent years within mainline denominations where decisions were made for them by superiors often quite removed from them in the religious hierarchy. Suddenly these people discovered that as the Comforter or Paraclete came to live on the inside, they had direct access to the mind of the Father. They discovered the reality of Jesus' promise that all of His sheep could hear His voice. The pendulum swung to the opposite extreme in an emphasis upon guidance for the individual from within. After all, does the new covenant not promise that all shall know Him for themselves— from the least to the greatest?

During our thirty years pastoring a large local church in metropolitan Detroit, we have lived through these same pendulum swings. We have learned through experience the necessity of balance in the area of guidance. That balance is provided in a proper understanding of the local church and of its pastor-shepherd. Guidance is not only individual, but corporate. Individual direction will be confirmed or corrected by what God is doing within the whole flock, if the sheep is rightly related to his local fold.

Along with the excitement of the widespread outpouring of the Holy Spirit upon people from all kinds of backgrounds, God is bringing to light many long-dormant doctrinal issues. Not only has He restored New Testament emphasis upon the sacraments and the reading of the Scriptures, but He has unearthed many questions regarding church government that have long been "on the shelf." As the Holy Spirit "leads into all truth," He does not conveniently by-pass all the issues we have found divisive. Instead, He presses for a resolution of these questions and a restoration of New Testament practice. As a part of this process of restoration, we experience readjustments and even consternation. But as long as we accept controversy as a part of healthy movement toward wholeness in the body of Christ, we can welcome the spotlight even on touchy questions such as shepherding and discipleship, and the purpose of the local church. Through it all we will come to an understanding of what God is saying to His people.

In his book we are presenting what the Lord has taught us as a local church during forty years' pioneering in building a strong and large local congregation. We are an independent local church, meaning that we have no headquarters or denominational backing. Those of us who lead have learned to follow the direction of Jesus Christ as our only head. When we speak of the ministry as an extension of Christ's shepherding, we are talking about something that is real to us. We have been forced to discover in daily experience the reality of that vital union with the Great Shepherd which alone makes us able ministers of the new covenant—genuine pastor-shepherds.

In the pages which follow, I hope to share with you what we have learned as a local congregation. I have given many personal observations in the hope that sharing from the vantage point of the large local assembly, we will add needed perspective. It is my contention that the local church is not an institution of the past, but is rather only now coming into its own as God's redeemed community in the earth. It is within the local fold that the pastor-shepherd finds his proper place in the body of Christ, not off in a corner of some living room. The shepherd belongs with his sheep in the local fold.

YOUR PASTOR, YOUR SHEPHERD

CHAPTER 1

God Is a Shepherd

I stood at the fence observing the sheep huddled at the far end of the paddock when my attention was distracted by a sharp whistle. I turned to see a large man, probably in his sixties, whistling through his teeth in successive short blasts. He was calling his dog. Behind me I heard a commotion.

The dog—a medium-sized German shepherd—came bounding from a wire-fenced kennel, gaining speed with each stride. Gathering momentum, he left the ground and soared magnificently over the wooden gate—with at least two foot clearance. His paws flailed for traction as they touched down. The dirt flew as he regained his stride. In moments he had worked his way behind the flock and was moving them toward us.

The dog raced back and forth in a loose figure eight behind the sheep without a bark or growl. The only sound in this pastoral scene, set in the rolling hills some fifty miles south of Auckland, New Zealand, was the wind singing through the lines of cedar trees that served as windbreaks along the fields and pastures. Another whistle. The dog stopped. The sheep began to mill quietly in front of us.

The man—an old Scot who looked every bit the storybook

shepherd—called the dog off. After a pat on the head, a rub, and a "good show," the dog raced away leaping the fence again, returned contentedly to his place.

In a matter of moments the flock was moving; one sheep started, the others followed. They chose another spot. There was no particular reason for it. One sheep stopped; the others followed suit. Within a few minutes the flock had moved again. They were following the aimless wandering of one sheep.

The old Scot whistled again. Another, but younger dog came humping eagerly from the kennel. The whistle was his signal to bark as well as to run. He, too, attempted to leap the fence, but he didn't time his jump as well as his partner had. His forepaws cleared, but his hind quarters hit the top rail with a crack. Undaunted, he hunched his hind legs up and pushed off into the paddock. The sheep heard him coming. They turned and slowly started to trot back to the shepherd.

Another whistle. The barking dog stopped and sidled up to the Scot, nuzzling his hand. After a pat on the head and word of approval, he saucily pranced back to the kennel. Moments later, the old Scot whistled to him again. He went into an adjoining paddock to encourage a solitary wandering sheep to return to the flock.

My attention returned to the flock. It was straying again. Off they went, head to tail, following the leader.

The next whistle alerted a third dog whose method was different. He knew which sheep had emerged from the butting order to be the leaders in the flock. By cutting them out and urging them toward the shepherd, this dog knew that the others would instinctively follow.

This Scot had things organized. In minutes he could move hundreds of sheep wherever he wanted them. The old shepherd knew his dogs and their abilities, and he used them to full advantage. That taught me something about the administration of a local—or parish—church.

Isaiah said: "All we like sheep have gone astray; we have turned every one to his own way . . ." (53:6). It is not a compliment to be compared with sheep. Sheep are stupid, ill-behaved and wayward. That's why they need a shepherd. Only the shepherd and his well-trained assistants kept the sheep together in a flock and in the pasture designated for grazing. The sheep were incapable of leading themselves.

The Scot could not have done the job by himself. His flock numbered about seven thousand sheep. He needed assistance. But the dogs also needed the shepherd. The dogs could not train themselves nor did they have the wisdom to care for the flock.

The animals were trained to bring the sheep to the shepherd that he might minister to their more intimate needs. The sheep remained quiet and calm while the shepherd spoke. As he did, he would rub one sheep, then look over another. As he moved among the sheep, they were alert and listening. But some minutes after he stopped, they grew restless and soon returned to wandering.

The Lord, My Shepherd

When David was keeping sheep on the hillsides of Palestine a long time ago, he apparently learned a similar lesson. He recognized how much like sheep we are. He also discovered that he had someone looking after him who was deeply concerned for his welfare. God was, in fact, taking care of him in the same way he was watching over his sheep. David exclaimed:

> The Lord is my shepherd. . . . (Psa. 23:1)

David was speaking as one of the sheep of God. Indeed, he was speaking for every child of God. Jesus Christ is our Shepherd, and we need His shepherding ministry. If we leave Him and wander off on our own, we do so to our own harm and hurt.

The compound names of God in Scripture all reveal God as the one who meets our needs. When God told Moses at the burning bush that His name was "I am that I am," He was really saying in effect, "Whatever you need Me to be, I will be to you."

Throughout the Old Testament God appeared to men during times of need and revealed how He was exactly what they needed. This process of unveiling culminated in the name of "Jesus," which means God is my salvation.

Jehovah-ra'ah means the Lord is my shepherd. David knew, from tending literal sheep and from observing his own waywardness, that we needed someone to tend us. We needed God to become to us all that a shepherd is to his sheep: leader, protector, provider, friend, corrector. David was expressing deep assurance of personal care when he realized that he had his very own shepherd. He had someone vitally concerned about him and able to lead him.

Jesus, as we know, is the Good Shepherd. Mark tells us that "Jesus . . . saw much people, and was moved with compassion toward them, because they were as sheep not having a shepherd: and he began to teach them many things" (6:34). His teaching was food for their souls. But when the multitudes became physically hungry, He trained His future successors to be shepherds by telling them to distribute loaves and fishes. And, in the early church, shepherds began their training by waiting tables (Acts 6:1-7).

Jesus knew that His sheep would scatter, just as John the Baptist's had, if He did not prepare them for His coming violent death. He would die, although He would not be absent for long. But He knew that, since they were sheep, they would be offended. "All ye shall be offended because of me this night: for it is written, I will smite the shepherd, and the sheep shall be scattered. But after that I am risen, I will go before you into Galilee" (Mark 14:27-28).

Peter insisted he would do better. He would be loyal to the death. But, like any other sheep when its shepherd is attacked, Peter was offended and took to straying.

God understands us. He made us the way we are, with the need for shepherding. This is part of our God-given capacity to respond to the Lord. Jesus knew that after His ascension into heaven the sheep would scatter again. His invisible ministry was not sufficient; they needed someone they could see. For this reason, He instituted a continuing ministry among His people, an extension of His own shepherding.

He Gave Pastor-Shepherds

The present shepherding ministry of Jesus is through flesh and blood men like me. I am a shepherd—actually, an undershepherd. Christ is the Great Shepherd and I work with Him and for Him. Shepherds, such as myself, are presently called "pastors," but both words mean the same thing. In this book, I will use the term "pastor-shepherd" to designate those persons who are called and separated by the Lord to gather the sheep of God into folds and flocks and care for them.

When Jesus ascended into heaven, He sent the Holy Spirit to dwell within the lives of His people. This advent of the Holy Spirit added a new dimension to human life. But, in addition to the gift of the Holy Spirit (Acts 2:38) to every believer, Christ also gave gifted men and women to His sheep. "And he gave some, apostles; and some, prophets; and some, evangelists; and some, pastors and teachers" (Eph. 4:11).

This does not mean that He gave some men the gift of apostleship, but that He gave men themselves to be apostles. All may prophesy and many have the gift of prophecy, but some persons are themselves prophets. When God gave pastors to His sheep, He gave them men and women who were shepherds. They had the requisite qualities.

In giving people as gifts to His sheep, Jesus was giving himself. In Hebrews 3:1, Jesus is called, "the Apostle and High Priest of our profession." As apostle, He is the great church planter and builder. And He was the great prophet spoken of by Moses in Deuteronomy 18:15. The Lord would speak through Him and the people were commanded to hearken to His words.

Furthermore, Jesus was God's evangelist. He said: "The Spirit of the Lord is upon me, because he hath anointed me to preach the gospel to the poor; he hath sent me to heal the brokenhearted, to preach deliverance to the captives, and recovering of sight to the blind, to set at liberty them that are bruised, to preach the acceptable year of the Lord'' (Luke 4:18-19).

Nicodemus, a ruler of the Jews, told Jesus, ''Rabbi, we know that thou art a teacher come from God. . .'' (John 3:2). Jesus' teaching differed from that of most of His contemporaries in that ''he taught . . . as one having authority, and not as the scribes'' (Matt. 7:29) who only mouthed the traditions of men.

Finally, Jesus identified himself as the pastor-shepherd in John 10. There he contrasted the good shepherd who lays down his life for the sheep with the hireling who flees at the approach of the wolf.

Jesus was and is our apostle, prophet, evangelist, pastor, and teacher. And He has sent gifted persons to His church to minister in each of these ways. They have always been in the church and they will continue with us until we have all reached full maturity in Christ.

CHAPTER 2

Jesus, the Bishop

Jesus Christ is a shepherd. He is also the Shepherd of shepherds. Jesus epitomizes all that a shepherd could ever be. He came to gather the lost sheep and to train shepherds to perpetuate His work. He came to demonstrate what a shepherd should be.

Four New Testament references emphasize different aspects of Christ's shepherding. All four are essential to the well-being of His sheep.

(1) He is the "Good Shepherd" who gives His life for the sheep (John 10:11).

(2) He is the "Great Shepherd" who went beyond death and rose to majestic life in order to go on caring for His sheep (Heb. 13:20-21).

(3) He is the "Shepherd and Bishop" of our souls—the only one who can restore us and make of us the true sheep of the Father (1 Pet. 2:24-25).

(4) He is the "Chief Shepherd" to whom all undershepherds must give account (1 Pet. 5:1-4).

These four essential elements of Christ's shepherding ministry can be summarized as: redemption, resurrection, restoration, and reward. They are exercised by the Son of God through the Holy Spirit and qualified men.

The Good Shepherd

A genuine pastor-shepherd differs from one who merely tends sheep because he has a heart for his sheep. He becomes everything to them: the source of water, food, protection, health, friendship—everything! And the sheep express their growing love and appreciation by an increasing dependent trust and careful following.

The good pastor-shepherd will, if necessary, lay down his life for the sheep. Most people put themselves first; but the pastor-shepherd puts the sheep first. F.B. Meyer wrote about Jesus:

> He has a shepherd's heart, beating with pure and generous love that counted not His life-blood too dear a price to pay down as our ransom. He has a shepherd's eye, that takes in the whole flock, and misses not even the poor sheep wandering away on the mountains cold. He has a shepherd's faithfulness, which will never fail nor forsake, nor leave us comfortless, nor flee when He seeth the wolf coming. He has a shepherd's strength, so that He is well able to deliver us from the jaw of the lion, or the paw of the bear. He has a shepherd's tenderness; no lamb so tiny that He will not carry it; no saint so weak that He will not gently lead; no soul so faint that He will not give it rest. (*The Shepherd Psalm,* p. 22)

Jesus revealed His shepherd-heart in His intimate prayer immediately before His arrest, trial and execution.

> My plea is not for the world, but for those you have given me because they belong to you; And all of them, since they are mine, belong to you; and you have given them back to me with everything else of yours, and so they are my glory! Now I am leaving the world, and leaving them behind, and coming to you. Holy Father, keep them in

> your own care—all those you have given me—so that they will be united just as we are, with none missing. During my time here I have kept safe within your family all of these you gave me. I guarded them so that not one perished. . . . (John 17:9-12 TLB)

Sheep do not stay together naturally. They are prone to wander and are easily scattered. Once separated from the flock and out of earshot from the shepherd, it is most difficult, if not impossible, for them to find their way back. Sheep will not remain together except when carefully guarded by a pastor-shepherd and his dogs. Unity without a shepherd? Impossible! The nature of the sheep demands that there be a shepherd.

But Jesus prayed for more than protection and unity. His sheep needed to grow into His likeness as well.

> They are not part of this world any more than I am. Make them pure and holy through teaching them your words of truth. As you sent me into the world, I am sending them into the world, and I consecrate myself to meet their need for growth in truth and holiness. (John 17:16-19 TLB)

How would His sheep develop? Only through constant exposure to His personal leadership. The pastor-shepherd must dedicate all he is—his time, his personality, his power of influence, even his personal goals—to the nurturing of the sheep. Shepherding demands this kind of consecration. It was not unusual for a shepherd to give his life, or at least risk it, for the sake of the sheep. David confronted a bear and a lion to save his flock.

The Great Shepherd

The Father answered the Good Shepherd's prayer by making Jesus the Great Shepherd. Christ's resurrection and ascension make it possible for Him to mature His people. He says:

> Now the God of peace, that brought again from the dead our Lord Jesus, that great shepherd of the sheep, through

> the blood of the everlasting covenant, make you perfect in every good work to do his will, working in you that which is wellpleasing in his sight, through Jesus Christ; to whom be glory for ever and ever. Amen. (Heb. 13:20-21)

Until Jesus suffered and died for our redemption, His ministry was limited. He performed miracles when personally present, and at times sent a healing word some distance through faith. But His influence was primarily upon those who could see and hear Him. His body was a human body like ours, with the same physical limitations. His power was in His words.

God did not intend for His presence to be confined forever to one human body, any more than He intended to remain enclosed in the little box the Bible calls "the ark of the covenant." God's heart of redeeming love is too big; He must reach everyone. Jesus had to come again without human limitations. This He did, once the purpose of His incarnation was accomplished. Jesus returned in the person of the Holy Spirit. This is why Jesus told His disciples that it was to their advantage for Him to go away; His ascension to the Father would open a whole new dimension of intimacy.

> Nevertheless I tell you the truth; it is expedient for you that I go away: for if I go not away, the Comforter will not come unto you; but if I depart, I will send him unto you. (John 16:7)

The Comforter was not a substitute to placate His bereaved followers; He was the Paraclete who would make the presence of Jesus available down inside each of them. The Holy Spirit was "another" Comforter—one exactly like Jesus. The Spirit of the Shepherd was to come into the sheep and remain. This is what Jesus had been telling His disciples as He prepared them for this transition. He reassured them that they would not be abandoned (John 14:16-18).

Before His transition into glory, Jesus could only exercise influence from the outside, but through the coming of the Holy

Spirit, He gained access to the inner recesses of the human personality. He could change His people from the inside out. Redemption brought more than salvation from God's wrath; it made possible basic character change through the inner working of the Holy Spirit. Jesus could personally superintend each individual sheep—from the inside.

The Shepherd and Bishop

Jesus carried the iniquities of the human race to the cross, paying the full penalty for them. Subsequently He could enter the depths of the personality to effect permanent change and remove the root of the waywardness.

> Who his own self bare our sins in his own body on the tree, that we, being dead to sins, should live unto righteousness: by whose stripes ye were healed. For ye were as sheep going astray; but are now returned unto the Shepherd and Bishop of your souls. (1 Pet. 2:24-25)

The work of conversion is carried on by shepherds. This does not simply mean leading people to an altar and introducing them to a savior who will wash them deeply from sin and give them a new start. Yes, we must begin there. But the real work of shepherding begins as soon as the lambs are born.

The word "bishop" emphasizes the responsibility of the shepherd to watch over the sheep. It comes from the Greek, *episkopos*, which means "overseer, inspector, or guardian." This spiritual oversight is a grave responsibility. To raise a lamb into a ram or a ewe the pastor-shepherd must tend each one throughout every important stage in its development.

Peter described the sheep before they returned to the Shepherd and Bishop of their souls as "going astray." The Greek implies that they were the victims of deliberate deception. They had been misled. Apart from the care of Jesus and His undershepherds, these sheep were being deceived, seduced, and made to err. The adversary had worked to create a flock of his own.

The genuine undershepherd must teach his sheep to follow only the voice of the true Shepherd. Depending upon how much harm the individual has experienced in his previous background, this may require considerable time and energy. But one fact is certain: all sheep have gone astray and need restoration (Isa. 53:6).

The Chief Shepherd

Pastor-shepherds do not own their own flocks. They are stewards of the Chief Shepherd. Stewards care for the property of others to whom they must give a detailed account. Because pastor-shepherds are responsible to Jesus Christ as stewards they may safely be trusted with our souls. If they did not have to give account, we would have reason to be wary of them. Our safety lies not in their inherent integrity, but in the watchfulness of Christ.

The more responsibility God gives us, the more He requires of us. Pastor-shepherds will be judged more severely than the average sheep. James warned: Let not many of you become teachers, my brethren, for you know that we who teach shall be judged with greater strictness" (James 3:1 RSV).

Power corrupts. Great leaders in all ages have destroyed themselves and their followers because they became drunk on the wine of their power influence. Undershepherds are exposed to the same temptation, but their special accountability to the Chief Shepherd exerts a keeping power over them. Peter puts it this way:

> The elders which are among you I exhort, who am also an elder, and a witness of the sufferings of Christ, and also a partaker of the glory that shall be revealed: feed the flock of God which is among you, taking the oversight thereof, not by constraint, but willingly; not for filthy lucre, but of a ready mind; neither as being lords over God's heritage, but being ensamples to the flock. And when the chief Shepherd shall appear, ye shall receive a crown of glory that fadeth not away. (1 Pet. 5:1-4)

Peter knew it is easy to become a kingdom-builder rather than a steward. It is more natural to use relationships to feed ourselves in one way or another than to feed others. We all love attention and applause—the thrill of knowing that many people take us seriously. And who doesn't at one time or another crave more money? We will fall into these dark paths unless we are deterred from without. But nothing on earth is strong enough to curb our human perversities; this requires the activity of the Chief Shepherd himself.

The Apostle Paul said:

> . . . we make it our aim to please him. For we must all appear before the judgment seat of Christ, so that each one may receive good or evil, according to what he has done in the body. Therefore, knowing the fear of the Lord, we persuade men; but what we are is known to God. . . . (2 Cor. 5:9-11 RSV)

The most helpless little lamb is safe in the arms of a pastor-shepherd who knows he is transparent before the Chief Shepherd.

All four of these facets of shepherding should be apparent in the church. Good shepherds will lay their lives down for the sheep. They will cooperate with the Holy Spirit to bring change to people's inner lives and relationships. They will restore and reeducate the sheep until they are content to remain in the fold and to follow their Shepherd and Bishop all the way. They will deal with God's people conscientiously because the Chief Shepherd will judge their stewardship.

CHAPTER 3

The Source of All Authority

In Paul's letter to the Ephesians we see the church as the fulness of Christ (chapter 1), "one new man" (2:11-18), the temple of God (2:19-22), as God's family (chapter 3), as in union with Christ (chapter 4), as the bride of Christ (chapter 5), and as God's army (chapter 6).

These seven important pictures all say the same thing about the church. They tell us that Christ is so intimately involved in His people that He is in reality present and active in the church upon the earth. Christ Himself is the source of the church's life and power. His own presence activates all that is accomplished. He is not a distant landlord, running things from "the great somewhere." He is the active, present head of His body. He and His people are "one," as He prayed they would be (John 17). He is still the Shepherd of His shepherds and of His sheep.

Christ became the head of the church when He ascended. He had first descended to remove all opposition to His supreme authority. He had then risen from the dead to be declared the Son of God (Rom. 1:4). But those events were not fulfilled until Christ ascended to the right hand of His Father—the place of all authority. This reign is evident now only to those who believe. But, one day, all nations, tribes and tongues will bow the knee to Him. Meanwhile the Great Shepherd is in the midst of those called out from the world to be His sheep. In His sheepfold, the church, we can expect to see His continued leadership.

A Covenant with a Shepherd King

Christ's exaltation fulfilled God's promise to the ancient king who had been a shepherd, David. On the day of Pentecost, Peter explained the resurrection and ascension in terms of Psalm 110—a psalm of David. In Paul's first recorded sermon, we find a fully developed connection between God's covenant with David and Christ's exaltation:

> And as concerning that he raised him up from the dead, now no more to return to corruption, he said on this wise, I will give you the sure mercies of David. Wherefore he saith also in another psalm, Thou shalt not suffer thine Holy One to see corruption. (Acts 13:34-35)

What are the sure mercies of David? They refer to the unbreakableness of the oath God gave to David. "My covenant will I not break, nor alter the thing that is gone out of my lips. Once have I sworn by my holiness that I will not lie unto David. His seed shall endure for ever, and his throne as the sun before me" (Psa. 89:34-36).

King David wanted to build a temple for the Lord. But God had other plans. David was a man of war: he was not suited for the task of building a temple. God instead chose David's son, Solomon, to do the actual building. He would give David the pattern, but the temple would be called Solomon's.

But it was David's more distant descendant, Jesus Christ, who would build the spiritual temple—the church. David's desire to erect a literal temple spoke of a greater glory to come, a spiritual habitation of praise from the lives of surrendered people (Eph. 2:19-22).

David wanted to build a house for God, but God purposed to

build a house for David. The term "house" in this instance meant lasting dynasty, a rule that would never end through David's descendants. God sent the prophet Nathan to spell out the terms of His covenant. "Thus saith the LORD of hosts, I took thee from the sheepcote, even from following the sheep, that thou shouldest be ruler over my people Israel" (1 Chron. 17:7). God and David were both shepherds. They knew about tending sheep.

The Davidic covenant contained four basic provisions and only one condition. God promised to give David: (1) "a house" — posterity; (2) "a throne"—authority; (3) "a kingdom"—a sphere of rule; and (4) "everlasting mercies"—continuance. But if any of David's seed became rebellious, God would punish them. But their failure could not nullify the covenant, and it was ultimately fulfilled in Christ, the son of David (Luke 20:41-44, etc.). Because Christ lives forever, He became the sure mercies of David. These sure mercies mean that we, as sheep, will never be left without leadership. Isaiah prophesied: "Incline your ear, and come unto me: hear, and your soul shall live; and I will make an everlasting covenant with you, even the sure mercies of David. Behold, I have given him for a witness to the people, a leader and commander to the people (55:3-4).

This covenant was confirmed to Mary when the angel delivered this message, "And, behold, thou shalt conceive in thy womb, and bring forth a son, and shalt call his name JESUS. He shall be great, and shall be called the Son of the Highest: and the Lord God shall give unto him the throne of his father David: And he shall reign over the house of Jacob for ever; and of his kingdom there shall be no end" (Luke 1:31-33).

Jesus' kingdom is not outward and visible, but has already begun in the hearts of those who have willingly surrendered to His lordship. Peter outlined the basic steps one must take to enter the sphere of Christ's rule: "Repent, and be baptized every one of you in the name of Jesus Christ for the remission of sins, and ye shall receive the gift of the Holy Ghost" (Acts 2:38). Christ joins us to himself spiritually, and to all others who likewise come to Him. We become a "member in particular" of His body. Joining the church means becoming an active participant in the power of Christ's ascension and present rule. But one cannot make himself into a follower; he must be inwardly drawn, forgiven, and changed by the sovereign working of the Holy Spirit. He must be "added" to the church (Acts 2:41, 47, etc.). We become God's inheritance when we become sheep who submit to a shepherd and remain within the flock.

Local sheepfolds are formed because of the work of the Spirit to raise up leaders who would gather the sheep. People living for themselves, loners at loose ends, suddenly find themselves drawn to commit themselves to a larger group because they sense leadership, the charisma (Spirit's gift) of leadership. We become unified under a leader.

CHAPTER 4

So You Want to Be a Shepherd?

Many people have been to church all their lives without really knowing what a pastor-shepherd is. They have called various men and women "pastor," but without understanding the special place this local minister should have in their lives.

A shepherd is distinct from all other agricultural laborers because of the nature of his work. Likewise a pastor is distinguished from apostles, prophets, evangelists, and teachers (see Ephesians 4:11) because of what he does and how he does it. We can observe at least four important differences:

(1) The pastor is responsible for a particular flock.
(2) He establishes relationships of personal involvement with individuals.
(3) He seldom develops a widespread reputation of the specialist, but confines himself to local concerns.
(4) Seeing his sheep develop toward maturity is his main reward in life.

Responsibility to a Fold

God gives a pastor to the people he or she serves. Whether you are a pastor-shepherd or one of the sheep, belonging to a sheepfold implies responsibility. It is a mutual relationship. If you belong to a local church, you not only belong to God but to the rest of the sheep in the fold.

The pastor-shepherd's responsibility to the sheepfold is like that of a head of a family. I am a husband and father. As an adult, I should be able to do what I want to do. If I get up tomorrow morning and feel like going to Arizona, I ought to be able to pack my bag and shove off. Wouldn't that be grand? But I cannot. I no longer live to myself. I must make my decisions in terms of the needs of those of whom I am a part—my wife and children.

I have also been called by God to be a pastor. That involves responsibilities as binding as those toward my own family. I cannot pick up and leave my sheep any more than I can walk out on my wife. No matter how attractive a spur-of-the-moment move to Arizona might sound, my commitment to the sheep rules it out.

Regrettably, many pastor-shepherds do not consider these matters carefully enough when they are weighing opportunities for their own personal advancement. Often they consider themselves free men who can go anywhere and do whatever seems to their advantage.

I do not believe that a pastor-shepherd can leave his flock by simply claiming that God whispered in his ear. We have seen too much of this. God's people must not be abandoned and left to the wolves. And if a change in leadership is in order, the flock must be left in the care of a successor who knows and cares about the sheep. Israel would have panicked when its leadership was being transferred to Joshua from Moses if they had not been thoroughly acquainted with Joshua. The people knew his gifts, temperament, and his love for them. And Moses did not stand on a sabbath morning and announce his resignation to a stunned flock. Sometime prior to the actual day of transition, Moses had laid his hands upon Joshua in the presence of the elders and the entire congregation.

You don't have to travel far in our nation to discover churches without adequate pastoral care. Literally thousands of pulpits stand empty and the sheep are either starving or scattered because the pastor-shepherd who once served the local sheepfold left them without a proper successor and genuine God-given oversight. Is it any wonder that congregations in so many localities are weak and dying, and perhaps even dead?

Relationships with Real People

Just as a shepherd knows each of his sheep by name, so the pastor is acquainted with each one of his people. No one is just a name or a handshake or a tithe account. Each person has a face, a personality, and a special place in his heart.

The church I pastor is large and sometimes people ask me, "How could you know the names of 3,000 sheep?" But I have a simple reply.

"I am involved with these people all the time. I see them come into the church. I watch them as they make their way to the altar and find God's grace. I see them enter the waters of baptism. I hear their radiant testimonies of discovering the reality of the baptism in the Holy Spirit.

"I sit at their dinner tables. I talk with their children. I dedicate their babies. I marry their young people. I bury their dead. I help them with the family budget when the going gets rough. It never ends."

This is what it means to tend sheep. Not unlike the family doctor, the pastor serves everyone in the family. Specialists can perform medical miracles the old G.P.s never dreamed of, but they are impersonal. They do not get acquainted with people as people, but as a circulatory system, a pair of eyes, a lower G.I. tract, etc. But we still need the personal touch of the family doctor. He knows when to refer us to a specialist. Similarly, the pastor-shepherd may refer one of his sheep to a specialist in deliverance, or healing, or counseling in a particular area. By doing that he does not surrender his personal involvement. He finds out what happened. How did

God meet the need? He personally knows the ministry of the one to whom He sends anyone.

Above all, the term "pastor-shepherd" implies relationship. When you call me "Pastor," you are acknowledging a relationship—a living, growing relationship.

I do not have this kind of relationship with the whole family of God. The flocks in Germany do not know me. Nor do they in France. Even in nearby Toledo only a few people know me. But in Bethesda Missionary Temple, the people are my sheep, and I must work with them carefully. This does not mean that I begin to think of myself as the Chief Shepherd. I dare not lord it over God's heritage. But it does mean that my relationship and responsibility toward these people is unique.

As preachers, we who pastor learn quickly enough that we receive more honor when we are away from home. We can tell old stories and get away with them, use illustrations without having anyone throw rocks at us, and combine the best of any number of sermons. Consequently, we receive adulation of our new audience. But when we return home there is no parade or marching band.

This tends to give some pastor-shepherds an itch to travel. After all, they are such a precious gift that they simply must share themselves with the multitudes. But we need to shrink our heads to the size of our hats and remain where the Lord has put us.

I love compliments as well as the next person. In fact, I eat them up. Through the years a number of well-intentioned people have told me my ministry was just too great to be confined to one local church. I have been momentarily excited by such dazzling suggestions. But they were nonsense. Just because people like to hear me speak as I travel the country does not automatically bestow upon me an apostolic gift of travel. The Lord called me to be a pastor-shepherd. And if I have a lick of sense, that is where I will remain.

Money is a problem, too. What I do should not be done for the sake of gain. If it is, I become a hireling and everything depends upon how much I am paid. The sheep instinctively know it when this happens. If a shepherd doesn't have the interest of his sheep at heart, it doesn't make any sense to be a shepherd.

Not for Reputation

One time I attended a convention in Indiana. During the three days I was called to preach once.

Every time a certain young man saw me, I was eating. He had only heard me speak once. Finally he came to me and said, "Brother Beall, could I ask you a question?"

"Sure," I replied.

"What do you do for a job?"

"I'm a minister—a pastor."

"I know you're a minister, but what else do you do?"

"I don't do anything else; this is all I do."

His eyes grew wide with astonishment. "You mean that's all you do? What else do you do with your time?"

To him a pastor is someone who preaches one time in three days and eats all the rest of the time! Evidently this young man had the idea that it was great fun to pastor. How far from the facts he was. How little he knew of the immense responsibility and intense pressure involved in fulfilling this calling faithfully.

The pastorate is not an office anyone should seek for himself. In Bible days no one clamored for the task of shepherding sheep. The job was often assigned to the youngest son or one of the daughters. It was a menial and thankless task of endless routine. Day after day the shepherd heard only the incessant bleating of sheep that were totally dependent on his care. This can become extremely wearisome over a period of years. It is no less so with people.

Moses had been raised as a prince in Egypt. He had education and prestige. But when the call of God came to him, it cost him his position. And, soon, Moses found himself in an entirely different position.

In Midian, he could find no other job than that of a shepherd. This was considered an abomination to the Egyptians. Moses' father-in-law, Jethro, gave Moses the job of herding his sheep on the backside of the desert for forty long years. When the time came for Moses to lead Israel out of bondage, his pride had been broken. He was ready to do it for the sake of others and not for his own name.

Shepherding needed to be done, since most of the land was not suitable for much else. Enough grass for sheep will grow where more lush vegetation cannot thrive. But those who did the shepherding were not held in high esteem. When Samuel wanted to anoint a king from among Jesse's sons, it took Jesse quite a time before he recalled that he had one more son—David, out tending the sheep. When Jesus spoke of himself as the Good Shepherd, He put himself in a humble position.

CHAPTER 5

The Shepherd Is More than a Preacher

The first occupation to be mentioned after man was expelled from the Garden of Eden was of keeping sheep. The first shepherd, Abel, gives us an excellent introduction to what the Bible has to say about shepherds and, in turn, pastors.

". . . and Abel was a keeper of sheep . . .(Gen. 4:2).

The Hebrew word for "keeper" or "shepherd" is *ra'ah* which occurs about eighty times in the Old Testament. Its meaning includes not only watchful care and attention to the practical needs of the sheep, but personal companionship (see Psalm 122:8). The shepherd does not keep his sheep in some cold and impersonal way.

We "keep" something because we prize it or because it is otherwise dear to our hearts. Jesus keeps His Father's sheep and is careful not to lose any. Even one sheep is a priceless possession.

> All that the Father giveth me shall come to me; and him that cometh to me I will in no wise cast out. For I came down from heaven, not to do mine own will, but the will of him that sent me. And this is the Father's will which hath sent me, that of all which he hath given me I should lose nothing, but should raise it up again at the last day.

(John 6:37-39)

This is quite a commitment—"to lose nothing." But notice that Jesus was not saying this about everyone who followed Him around in the crowd, but about a certain select group—those His Father had given Him to keep as sheep. Those particular people would be called out of the world and personally come to Him; they would pick Him out as someone special and allow Him to matter to them. They would develop a special relationship to Him as their shepherd, and this relationship would "keep" them.

The pastor-shepherd cannot bear the thought of losing any of his sheep. As in the familiar parable (Luke 15:3-7; Matt. 18:12-14), he will leave the ninety-nine safe in the fold and go out to brave the elements in search of the one that has turned up missing. Each individual matters to him. He is not concerned only with numbers. He may have a large church, but if "dear Sister So-and-So" is not doing well, he is concerned. He must seek her out and deal with the matter.

We cannot "keep" something until we have first received it. The Father gave Jesus men and women who sought Him out and submitted to His care. But He in return had to receive them. Before he can allow a shepherd to keep him, a sheep must be assured of acceptance.

All of us fear rejection. Some of us have been deeply wounded in almost every relationship we have experienced—especially those with authority figures like parents, teachers, and employers. They can only be healed through a positive and lasting relationship. Being kept by a pastor-shepherd who is concerned for their good will restore their confidence in human authority and heal their fears about God who is the ultimate authority. The sheep that knows it is loved and valued is not easily lost.

Learning to Trust Takes Time

Countless people want to find a pastor they can trust. Hurt by someone who represented God in their past, they want to trust another spiritual leader but they are wary. So they sit and listen. They observe. They test your motives. They listen to the tone of your voice. They watch carefully how you deal with others, and sometimes only after years of this do they open their lives to the pastor for his ministrations.

I venture a guess: some folks have sat in our services for more than five years before they were able to trust me as their spiritual leader. When finally they made the plunge, they commented, "I declared I would never trust my life to another minister as long as I lived. I had to be sure about you."

I have discovered that there must be a mutual wanting in the shepherd-sheep relationship. The sheep must know he is wanted, and the pastor-shepherd must have the assurance that he has been accepted by the one who is to follow. This makes church membership more than a surface commitment; it is decisive spiritual living.

Jesus did not keep sheep for himself, but for His Father. Likewise, the undershepherds are keeping them in Jesus' name, as a responsibility both to God and to the people in their charge. But exactly how do they go about it? Isaiah lists five basic functions of the pastor-shepherd. Notice the italicized verbs in the following quotation:

> Behold, the Lord GOD will come with strong hand, and his arm shall *rule* for him: behold, his reward is with him, and his work before him. He shall *feed* his flock like a shepherd: he shall *gather* the lambs with his arm, and *carry* them in his bosom, and shall gently *lead* those that are with young. (40:10-11, italics mine)

The Shepherd Rules

Isaiah was certainly familiar with the habits of shepherds. He noticed the important place of the hand and arm in the work of shepherding. The shepherd uses his strong hand and arm both to defend the sheep from danger and to handle them when they need special attention. When Isaiah describes the Messiah as shepherd by saying "his arm shall rule for him," he is saying that his influence will come by means of his personal touch.

The laying on of hands is a common form of ministry throughout the New Testament as well as the Old. You will discover that basically it blossmed into its fulness in the ministry of Christ. Jesus was not afraid to touch people. And His touch was not always ecclesiastical. He was such a warm man that I think He must have put His arm around the shoulders of His apostles as He talked with them.

I have wondered just how the conversation went as He told Peter that Satan had desired to sift him like wheat, but He would be praying for him that his faith would not fail. My imagination says that He had His arm around his shoulder as they walked and talked. Jesus loved Peter and wouldn't do anything to hurt him. This sifting was necessary to Peter's growth. Jesus wanted him to know that he would not be out of his thoughts during this unpleasant ordeal.

I have watched men and women blossom after I told them that they were coming along splendidly. Just holding the the hand after you have shaken it can speak volumes. A hand on the shoulder as you are walking toward the door can convey a warmth the sheep desperately need. People nuzzle up to you like a house dog who desires to have his nose scratched, his back rubbed, or his ears affectionately pulled. I find it difficult to be a thundering preacher of the judgment of God while stroking the ears of the sheep.

The Hebrew word for rule in this passage in Isaiah speaks of dominion, of governing, of reigning with power. The shepherd is in charge of the flock. He makes the decisions and the sheep follow him; it is not the other way around. His rule is an extension of Christ's.

As pastor-shepherd of a local church, I am responsible for what happens. It must be my business to know what is going on and to be sure that I approve of it. I will have to give account to the Chief

Shepherd. If I permit anything against my conscience without speaking up, it will be my fault.

When I in turn delegate authority to others, I must maintain that personal touch. My arm must rule for me. I must know those I put in any position of authority, but I must also keep in touch with them. It is part of my duty to be sure they are carrying out the instructions I gave them, but with kindness and consideration.

The Shepherd Feeds

The Greek verb *poimaino* was used both literally and figuratively by the New Testament writers. Its basic meaning is "herd," "tend," or "(lead to) pasture" (Arndt and Gingrich). But they also employed it with reference to the church to describe activity that protects, rules, governs, and fosters. A shepherd, in Greek, is a *poimen*, one who actually does the job. Nothing—not education, not talent, not ecclesiatical appointment—will suffice to make a true shepherd of a person who does not have a heart for the job. The man who leads the flock to green pastures is, in the end, the one to whose voice they will listen.

It often happens that aspiring young seminary and Bible school graduates begin their careers as assistants to the pastors of larger congregations. Almost as often these aspiring ministers are talented, delightful people to whom the parishioners respond to warmly. Teamed with the senior minister, they make a powerful team. In that position, however, they are sorely tempted to think they've got what it takes. Put that together with the tiresomeness of being number two and you've frequently got a young person looking for a flock he can call his own. Many apparently succeed.

Too late they discover that, although they can preach, pray, sing, visit and play the piano with the best of them, they cannot feed their sheep adequately. In time the flock is lean and irritable, and the young pastor begins to take it personally. He learns an old axiom the hard way—if you can't feed them, they won't follow you.

Radio ministers who repeatedly ask for money are those who offer no real spiritual food. People know it and simply do not support the program. The minister can cry and make one appeal after another, and even resort to gifts and gimmicks, but it is only a matter of time until the machinery grinds to a halt.

Spiritual food is a word within a word. It is your words conveying the thought, word, and direction given you by the Holy Spirit. He speaks, we listen; the word is digested and then framed in our vernacular. But nevertheless it had its origination in the mind of God. When the Lord said to Peter, "Feed my sheep," He meant for Peter to get his direction from the Holy Spirit and then to prepare his words so that his hearers would be able to understand in their language what the Lord wanted done. Feeding, to me, means the ability to articulate understandably the burden the Holy Spirit has placed upon your heart.

Shepherding is not arbitrary dictatorship; it is leading the sheep into pastures rich with food. Ruling is a necessary part of bringing the sheep to the food they need. Sheep cannot find their own food. They must be taken to the pastures. A responsible shepherd knows the terrain and the best routes to get from one pasture area to another. The sheep can only come to good grazing country by allowing themselves to be governed by someone who knows the way better then they do.

Again and again in Scripture we find shepherding related to feeding. Take these few examples:

> Feed the flock of God which is among you, taking the oversight thereof. . . . (1 Pet. 5:2)
>
> Take heed therefore unto yourselves, and to all the flock, over the which the Holy Ghost hath made you overseers, to feed the church of God. . . . (Acts 20:28)
>
> Let the elders that rule well be counted worthy of double honour, especially they who labour in the word and doctrine. (1 Tim. 5:17)

Sheep do not come to a pastor-shepherd to be dominated or

coerced; they come to be fed. Godly authority is a natural result of feeding the inspired word. The sheep will heed the voice they can trust and respect. They learn this trust because when they follow, they experience satisfaction. They are fed.

Sheep who are not led to new pastures will die of starvation. God's people cannot feed on one aspect of God's truth alone and expect to grow. Some pastor-shepherds ride a hobby horse of truth, that is, they take one particular truth of the Bible and ride it to death. Some do it with justification by faith, others with water baptism, still others with healing, others with their own brand of demonology, others with their theories on the tribulation and the millennium. The list could go on interminably. And, sooner or later, the sheep refuse to come to the table because they can no longer stomach mashed potatoes warmed over with gravy of another color poured over them.

A young man once engaged me in conversation. During our few minutes together, I asked him about his church. He said, "I belong to a 'fifty-and-two' church."

I said, "A what?"

He answered, "A fifty-and-two church."

I replied, "I don't have the faintest idea what you are talking about."

He smiled and explained, "A fifty-and-two church is one that preaches salvation fifty weeks in the year and tithing the other two."

The Shepherd Gathers

Sheep instinctively go astray. Gathering is one of the unique charismatic qualities the Lord gives to the pastor-shepherd. By it he becomes so appealing to sheep that they will gather around him. They will listen to him and follow his example. He is able to generate trust in sheep so that they can eat in peace and lie down with a feeling of safety.

Many people who can preach are not able to gather sheep. You can give them a church already established with several hundred people, but in six months they will have scattered the sheep. This is not because they did not know the Bible or could not communicate. It was because they lacked the personal qualities that make a pastor-shepherd a keeper of sheep.

Some people who preach simply repel sheep. Gathering is not among the gifts God has given to them. This does not mean that they do not have other needed gifts. It simply means that they will not be able to be the pastor-shepherd of a local church. Instead, they would be wise to work with someone who has already gathered the sheep. No pastor can tend the sheep alone. He needs others with varying gifts to assist him in caring for the sheep. Those who cannot gather should work with those who can.

I remember well some Bible classes I was conducting in Detroit among mostly new converts. In response to some of their questions I began a panoramic study of Daniel and Revelation. All went well until I had to leave town for two weeks to fulfill a preaching commitment. Before I left the city, I called a ministerial friend who was well acquainted with the subject we were pursuing. He agreed to take the class in my absence.

When I returned two weeks later, I didn't have a class. As I began to round up the sheep and to question as to their whereabouts, they told me, "I'll never understand that. I'm confused; I don't think I want to continue."

My friend knew all the Bible texts and theories, but he didn't have the slightest notion where the sheep were, or what diet they needed. I have endeavored not to make the same mistake again.

The Shepherd Carries

Sheep depend upon their shepherd. Their dependency grows out of an honest realization of personal need and builds on their trust in the shepherd. Sheep are helpless creatures. They cannot look out for themselves. God's people are much the same. The lambs, or newly born, are almost totally defenseless.

Isaiah says the shepherd will carry the sheep in his bosom. He will allow them to come close. This speaks of the personal attention all sheep need. When cold weather comes and a lamb has not yet grown a coat of protective wool, the shepherd shields it inside his own clothes from the blasts of wind and rain. The pastor-shepherd must make time to deal personally with people in special need.

People come to places in life where they cannot cope. They will lie down and give up if someone does not carry them over this rough spot. A pastor-shepherd cannot remain aloof to realistic needs. He interferes at times for the well-being of everyone. Lambs do grow up, and pastor-shepherds must be careful not to shelter the sheep beyond what is for their personal development. He must carry them in such a way that they want to grow up. But he does not leave them to fend for themselves until he knows they can.

The Shepherd Leads

Isaiah paints a beautiful picture when he says, "He shall gently lead those that are with young" (40:11). The female sheep are called ewes. These ewes become so pregnant that they cannot be driven far in one day or they will easily die of exhaustion.

For their sake, the shepherd must slow down the entire flock. They must all travel at the pace of the most needy member. This is what Jacob was talking about when he said to Esau: "The flocks and herds with young are with me: and if men should overdrive them one day, all the flock will die" (Gen. 33:13). The shepherd must watch his ewes carefully and be ready to help if they have any difficulty giving birth.

> He chose David also his servant, and took him from the sheepfolds: From following the ewes great with young he brought him to feed Jacob his people, and Israel his inheritance. (Psa. 78:70-71)

Shepherds in the East usually go before their sheep. But when the ewes are great with young, the situation is reversed. The shepherd patiently and gently encourages the mothers to go at a rate they can take, and he restrains the rest of the flock. Pace is important for sheep as it is for a runner or an automotive assembly line. Break the rhythm of life and you will create problems. Impetuousness can destroy this sense of pace.

A young man who had attended our church left because I was not preaching what he considered "Kingdom Truth." What this meant is not important. But it did reveal an attitude. In most churches and religious organizations there are people who consider themselves "the spiritual forerunners." They look down their noses at the poor folks who do not have their spiritual comprehension. But they are not workers, table waiters, or callers on the sick. Instead they busy themselves by eliminating song books from their churches, discontinuing Sunday school classes, canceling Sunday evening services, and on and on, because of their elitist feelings. A true pastor must gently oppose such people in order to protect the ewes with young.

The work of the pastor-shepherd requires a great deal of sensitivity to the differing needs of the sheep. At different stages of development, we need different things. The pastor-shepherd must know his sheep and anticipate their needs. The only way he can keep a flock is by satisfying the needs of each individual sheep.

CHAPTER 6

Serving—And Loving It

The shepherd is the leader of the flock because he serves the sheep. They would be helpless without him. And that creates special temptations. We all need to be needed. When people continually turn to us for advice and help, it is easy for us to stop thinking of ourselves as servants and to imagine we are really someone special.

Young and inexperienced leaders are especially vulnerable to this. They begin with untried ideas, fresh energy and youthful vision. And they think they will accomplish more by bossing others around than by serving them. They lay down strict rules and rigid requirements to ensure a prospering group.

When King Rehoboam succeeded Solomon, he began, as any new leader should, by calling in the advisors who had assisted his father. They were experienced in the affairs of state and could pass on valuable insights to the new ruler. Their advice was timely and wise:

> And they spake unto him, saying, If thou wilt be a servant unto this people this day, and wilt serve them, and answer them, and speak good words to them, then they will be thy servants for ever. (1 Kings 12:7)

Did Rehoboam recognize the soundness of this advice? Apparently not. He dismissed the men of experience and called for his personal friends. He asked counsel of his peers who were eager to gain favor by saying what the king wanted to hear. They urged him to do what he wanted to do—to lord it over the people. Rehoboam foolishly chose to drive and to bully the people. And, soon, an usurper, Jeroboam, convinced the ten northern tribes—whose loyalty to the Davidic dynasty was less strong—to revolt against Rehoboam and to make him their king. The plot succeeded and Solomon's heir was left only with the two tribes of Judah and Benjamin.

Jesus was well aware of the divisiveness produced by arbitrary leadership. Jesus spent three and a half years training His disciples to serve before He allowed them to carry on His ministry. They were too self-centered. Leadership did not mean telling everybody else what to do, but serving them, becoming an example, and drawing from them the loving response of submission.

Jesus' disciples disputed more than once about who would be their leader. Mark tells us James and John worked to get Jesus into a generous frame of mind and then requested positions of honor from Him. Jesus used the occasion to spell out the difference between what He meant by leadership and what the world system meant and means.

> But Jesus called them to him, and saith unto them, Ye know they which are accounted to rule over the Gentiles exercise lordship over them; and their great ones exercise authority upon them. But so shall it not be among you: but whosoever will be great among you, shall be your minister: and whosoever of you will be the chiefest, shall be servant of all. For even the Son of man came not to be ministered unto, but to minister, and to give his life a ransom for many. (Mark 10:42-45)

The Greek word for "minister" is more often translated as "servant." It is the word, *diakonos*, from which we derive "deacon" and "deaconess." It means: "to wait tables as an attendant, to carry out orders as a deputy for another, to give relief to those needing help, to supply the necessities of life, or to render friendly service." Our modern idea of a deacon is far removed from the Bible truth of serving, and our concept of ministry is even more distorted.

What Is a Servant?

The meanings of words change over the centuries. In the field of religion many words are "romanticized." We have painted spiritual auras around them. They no longer simply say something concrete, but are now freighted with emotional associations.

The various Bible words for servant either meant slave or employee. There was nothing sentimental or flowery about it. To serve meant to perform one's duty, to get a job done, or to accomplish something useful. Today we use the word "laborer" to convey the same idea.

> And Jesus went about all the cities and villages, teaching in their synagogues, and preaching the gospel of the kingdom, and healing every sickness and every disease among the people. But when he saw multitudes, he was moved with compassion on them, because they fainted, and were scattered abroad, as sheep having no shepherd. Then saith he unto his disciples, The harvest truly is plenteous, but the labourers are few; pray ye therefore the Lord of the harvest, that he will send forth labourers into his harvest. (Matt. 9:35-38)

Jesus had been into ministering to these people: teaching, preaching, healing, and graciously meeting individual human needs. But there was work to be done that He could not do personally because He was not free to remain in one place. Jesus needed co-workers to follow up what His personal visitation had begun in these people—co-workers who would do the day-to-day work of caring for the people.

God answered that prayer by sending the Holy Spirit among

men, making them gifted persons to serve others. Some of these gifted ministers initiated men and women into the kingdom, others performed specialized services, and still others tended them in the daily routine of life. The Apostle Paul considered all of these as "labourers together with God" (1 Cor. 3:5-10).

The Qualities of a Servant

Our religious use of the term "servant" is not too close to the biblical concept, but, surprisingly enough, the nonreligious usage has changed very little. Thus we can recover much of the biblical concept by examining Webster's dictionary.

(1) A servant is bound to do the bidding of his superior.
(2) A servant is a personal or domestic attendant who performs duties for the person in the home of his master.
(3) A servant functions as an instrument under direction.
(4) A servant is a subordinate who acts for his master.
(5) A servant is one who helps another in practical ways.
(6) A servant is one who takes care of the affairs or property of another.

We could summarize these qualities of the servant with six words: obedience, helpfulness, stewardship, submission, usefulness, and faithfulness. One day, Jesus' disciples were discussing a problem of what to do when offended by the actions or words of others. Jesus taught them to expect offenses and to forgive. We can pour out more forgiveness than people can pour in offense. But this is the case only when our faith continues to draw upon God's inexhaustible resources.

The disciples recognized that it is easier said than done. Consequently, they asked a practical question: "How do you get enough faith to keep on forgiving?"

Jesus answered, "It is not how much faith you have—a mustard seed will do; it is how you use it. It is your attitude! Are you serving in order to be praised or are you performing tasks in gratitude to a master who purchased you out of hard bondage?

> When a servant comes in from plowing or taking care of sheep, he doesn't just sit down and eat, but first prepares his master's meal and serves him his supper before he eats his own. And he is not even thanked, for he is merely doing what he is supposed to do. Just so, if you merely obey me, you should not consider yourselves worthy of praise. For you have simply done your duty. (Luke 17:7-10 TLB)

We shouldn't expect a medal for doing our duty. And the man in leadership who is constantly looking for praise and commendation puts himself in a dangerous position, because rebellious people are forever looking for a leader's weakness in order to attack him there. So, for more than one reason, we ought to seek to be lowly of heart so that when we obey God we won't be deceived into thinking we've done something extraordinary—only our duty.

Faith stimulates obedience which, in turn, increases our faith. When we perform a service because we believe He asked us to do it, we will be strengthened when we see Him provide the power to execute it. Faith "works"—becomes operative and effective—by love (Gal. 5:6). When we obey God because we love Him, He will help us serve others in love. And His love will consume the stings we feel when we're attacked before they can lodge on the inside of us. The key to God's protections is the realization that we are working for someone other than ourselves. And from that comes our freedom to completely give ourselves to the sheep.

The great English expositor and pastor, Charles Bridges, saw the glory of unselfish serving.

> There is no more responsible thought connected with our work, than the obligation of giving ourselves to our people, so that they shall be led to prize us as a gift from Christ. Oh! that we might be able to tell them, We belong to Christ, and he has given us to you; we owe our whole selves entirely to you; we are your servants for Jesus' sake; we have given ourselves to the work, and we

> desire to be in it, as if there was nothing worth living for besides: it shall form our whole pleasure and delight. We will consecrate our whole time, our whole reading, our whole mind and heart to this service. (*The Christian Ministry*, p. 106)

The Sheep Are My Delight

At the time of this writing, I have helped pastor the same church in Detroit for more than thirty years. I have come to love these people deeply. And I have endeavored to be an authentic pastor-shepherd—that is, a person who is not affected by his station or position. I want to be a person who loves others and can show it. You cannot fool the sheep about this. They know if we enjoy being with them. They are quick to perceive it if we shy from them or avoid them.

The same is true with children. They can readily tell whether or not you like them. And they will instinctively avoid those whom they sense are even remotely unfriendly. A good place to check the condition of your heart is with the youngsters of your congregation. Do they run up and hug your legs? Do you love it when the little girls show you their pretty dresses, and young fellows proudly display new pants and shoes?

When a pastor truly loves his flock and delights in them, it promotes godliness and righteousness. The sheep hesitate to do anything to damage that relationship, or to bring a cloud between themselves and the Lord. We love each other. It is our mutual delight to serve each other.

This desire to serve people, and to be with them, makes the difference between the genuine pastor-shepherd and the "preacher." The pastor-shepherd must genuinely like people. If he does not, his work will be drudgery instead of delight.

The Work of an Eastern Shepherd

Since we are seeking a truly biblical concept of shepherding, we should look more closely at the shepherds of the Middle East. More than the shepherds of Europe and America, he lives for and among his sheep. His is a more primitive existence and his relationship with the animals themselves is more intense and personal—characteristic of Arab-Semitic culture as against the more staid northern Europeans.

Shortly before dawn he leads his flock out to find pasture. Sheep eat enormous amounts of grass so that the shepherd must constantly be finding new pastures, often at considerable distance from home. By noon, he must find water for them and a place to rest during the heat of the early afternoon. Up again to more pasture after that and then back to the fold at night.

> In late autumn or winter months, there are times when the shepherd can find no pasturage that is available for his flock, and then he must become responsible for feeding the animals himself. If the flock is small there may be times when it is stabled within the peasant house, and the family lives on a sort of mezzanine floor above it. At such seasons of the year the shepherd must provide the food. . . . In some sections of Syria, flocks are taken at this season to places in the mountain country, where the shepherd busies himself with the bushy trees, cutting down branches that have green leaves or tender twigs that the sheep and goats can eat. (*Manners and Customs of Bible Lands*, P. 152)

Can you imagine a greater involvement in one's work? How many of us want to bring the concerns of our business of profession right into the home? Most of us prefer to leave our responsibilities at the office or shop door. This is not possible when raising sheep.

Shepherding is not only demanding, it is dangerous. Both natural and human enemies threaten the lives of the sheep and their shepherds. This is the case today as well as in ancient times. W.M. Thomson says:

> Many adventures with wild beasts occur not unlike that

> recounted by David, and in these very mountains; for, though there are now no lions here, there are wolves in abundance; and leopards and panthers, exceeding fierce, prowl about these wild wadies. They not infrequently attack the flock in the very presence of the shepherd, and the shepherd must be ready to do battle at a moment's warning. I have listened with intense interest to their graphic descriptions of downright and desperate fights with these savage beasts. And when the thief and robber come (and come they do), the faithful shepherd has often put his life in his hand to defend the flock. . . . A poor faithful fellow last spring, between Tiberias and Tabor, instead of fleeing, actually fought three Bedawin [Bedouin] robbers until he was hacked to pieces with their khanjars, and died among the sheep he was defending. (*The Land and the Book,* pp. 200-203)

Another less grievous problem that regularly confronts the shepherd comes when a ewe gives birth. It may happen on a cold mountainside or just when the flock is being prodded to ford a stream. The shepherd must rush to her aid, leaving the rest of the flock to fend for itself. Immediately after she licks off her lamb and has given it suck, the shepherd must protect the tiny creature from becoming chilled. It will be a few days before this little one will be able to walk. The shepherd cannot stop the whole flock until the lamb is ready to move with it. So, he carries the newborn lamb, warming it within his bosom. The shepherd's large cloak of thickly woven wool contains a pouch in the breast large enough for just this purpose.

But pregnant ewes are not alone in needing the special attention of the shepherd. Hostility can and does arise between members of the flock, disease strikes various ones, others become injured or lost. To deal with these problems he may be tempted to isolate the ones with a problem to more easily help them. We try the same idea today when we establish small groups for divorcees, young marrieds, the elderly, and so on. But experience teaches that just about everything should be kept within the setting of the whole flock. Only rarely and out of necessity should a shepherd isolate or otherwise remove one of the sheep from the flock.

The wise shepherd makes considerable use of his dogs and of his sling. With them he finds ways to meet most exigencies while the whole flock continues to move toward the day's goal. Sometimes he makes use of other sheep in helping. For example, he may find another ewe to nurse a newborn lamb if the mother is sick or dying. Sheep differ, and the experienced shepherd takes this in stride. Listen to W.M. Thomson again:

> As you mentioned at the Amur the other day, I notice that some of the flock keep near the shepherd, and follow withersoever he goes, without the least hesitation, while others stray about on either side, or loiter far behind; and he often turns round and scolds them in a stern, sharp cry, or sends a stone after them. I saw him lame one just now. (*The Land and the Book,* p. 202)

Within God's flock the Holy Spirit helps the pastor in marvelous ways. The pastor-shepherd will lead the whole flock into a fresh passage in the word, and the Spirit will apply it to each sheep according to his need. We must never neglect the regular teaching and preaching of the word. How many times in my experience as pastor-shepherd have I had people who, weeks before, had made appointments for counseling and then called to cancel because their particular need had been met in one of the regular services?

Sheep need constant supervision. The only practical way to maintain it is to keep them together as a flock. This requires ceaseless vigilance on the part of the shepherd. Such watchfulness can become wearisome, but it has its moments of joy and serenity, too. George M. Mackie records for us some of the happier scenes of shepherding:

> By day and by night the shepherd is always with his sheep. . . . As he is always with them, he is constantly

> providing for them. He is not only ready to protect them, but conducts them to the most suitable ground by the best way; gives them music on his reed flute, to which the younger ones sometimes respond by capering around him, strips leaves from the branches, leads them at noon to the shelter of a cliff, or to the shade of a walnut or willow tree beside the well or brook. . . . (*Bible Manners and Customs,* p. 33)

The shepherd's day closes when he brings the sheep back to the sheepfold for the night—unless it is his turn to keep watch at the door. He counts his sheep two by two as they pass under his rod or hands and checks them for wounds or illness. But if a sheep is missing, his work is not over—he must go out and find the last one.

CHAPTER 7

Guard that Door!

Sheep need considerable protection. God did not equip them with claws or sharp teeth, nor did He make them agile enough to outrun enemies or to climb trees to avoid dangers. Sheep need to be tended by shepherds who will protect them.

In addition to wild boars, wolves, leopards, lions, jackals, and snakes, sheep are preyed upon by men. The Bedouins (desert wanderers) lived by stealing sheep. The dangers from animals and men were greatest at night and so the shepherds gathered their flocks into folds. These were often little more than makeshift shelters. The shepherd sat at the door of the sheepfold to admit no one but those who belonged.

In the marketplace the sheep of various shepherds were herded into more elaborate common enclosures with high walls to keep out thieves and robbers. A porter guarded the door. He knew the lawful shepherds and admitted them. But he refused to admit others. A door is both a means of access and of exclusion.

Jesus may have been standing near one of the marketplace sheepfolds when He gave His discourse, recorded in John 10, about the Good Shepherd and himself as the Door. To understand Jesus' words as His immediate audience did, we must do a little digging.

Jesus had healed a man born blind (John 9). The Jewish leaders were not used to seeing God in action, for theirs was a religion of precept alone. They were angry at Jesus. Jesus used this occasion of controversy to compare himself with those who considered themselves the shepherds of God's people.

The Pharisees and scribes, according to Jesus, were blind. They themselves could not see what God wanted, and thus had no power to lead others. They had not entered into God's sheepfold by His appointment and calling, but "by some other way." They had taken the responsibility of shepherding upon themselves without God-given authority. They were not "gifts" to God's people, but thieves and robbers.

There is a difference between thieves and robbers. The thief is a sneak. He gets in when no one is watching, by deception. The robber, on the other hand, employs violence. He may carry weapons and work in bands with other robbers to outnumber the keepers of the fold. They come to plunder, destroy and take what they want for themselves. Neither the thief or the robber is likely to walk up to the front door, knock, and ask, "May I come in?"

Jesus, and those shepherds who work along with Him, enter legitimately by the door. The porter recognizes them and gladly gives them access to their sheep. God's approval will be apparent in the life of a man who has become a shepherd in obedience to God's call. The genuine pastor-shepherd enters his calling by identifying with Jesus Christ. He will first become a sheep, and then allow the Great Shepherd to develop him into a leader. He comes into the fold in exactly the same way all sheep come in—through Christ, the Door. "Verily, verily, I say unto you, He that entereth not by the door into the sheepfold, but climbeth up some other way, the same is a thief and a robber" (John 10:1).

Climbing up some other way no doubt requires much effort. It may entail years of schooling and preparation. But if this effort does not lead to personal encounter with Christ, the would-be minister can never be more than a thief or robber. The Holy Spirit will not add His unction to the words of any but those who have entered through Christ.

Sheep know the difference between a pastor-shepherd set over them by God and one who has gained the office by some other means. Jesus said, "But he that entereth in by the door is the shepherd of the sheep. To him the porter openeth; and the sheep hear his voice: and he calleth his own sheep by name, and leadeth them out" (John 10:2-3).

The sheep have the right to hear the voice of Jesus through their pastor-shepherd. They can also expect him to live righteously, godly, and soberly. He preaches and lives the truth of the gospel. He must daily experience the personal presence of Christ.

We have placed too much emphasis on education and too little on this crucial matter of personal piety in the preparation of ministers. We think that by sending a person to college and seminary, or Bible school, that we will have prepared him to be a pastor. And, inevitably, the small congregations which can ill afford the strain of inexperienced young pastors, are the ones that must nonetheless receive them. This is true regardless of the form of church government—episcopal, presbyterian, or congregational—since it is, sad to say, much more a matter of economics than anything else.

And what happens? After a time the people either compel their pastor to leave, or they themselves begin to leave. They know something is wrong, but they can't explain it. They just grow restless. It happens because their pastor is really a stranger who is not feeding his flock the words he has heard from God, but words that he has conceived in his own head or perhaps stolen from others. They often sound quite eloquent, but they cannot bestow life.

The Apostle Paul, after spending considerable time at Ephesus establishing the church there, departed with this solemn warning:

> And now, behold, I know that ye all, among whom I

> have gone preaching the kingdom of God, shall see my face no more. Wherefore I take you to record this day, that I am pure from the blood of all men. For I have not shunned to declare unto you all the counsel of God. Take heed therefore unto yourselves, and to all the flock, over the which the Holy Ghost hath made you overseers, to feed the church of God, which he hath purchased with his own blood. For I know this, that after my departing shall grievous wolves enter in among you, not sparing the flock. Also of your own selves shall men arise, speaking perverse things, to draw away disciples after them. Therefore watch, and remember, that by the space of three years I ceased not to warn every one night and day with tears. And now, brethren, I commend you to God, and to the word of his grace, which is able to build you up, and to give you an inheritance among all them which are sanctified. I have coveted no man's silver, or gold, or apparel. (Acts 20:25-33)

Paul had acted as a guardian—a sort of door—for the flock while the local shepherds were gaining maturity and experience. They worked with him to learn how to keep the doors closed to counterfeit ministers and false brethren. He had showed them the nature of a true pastor-shepherd in contrast to self-appointed deceivers in several ways:

(1) He had given them a balanced diet in the Scriptures (v.27).
(2) His warnings came out of personal investment in the sheep (v.31).
(3) He coveted no material gain, but preferred to be a giver (vv. 33-35).

In these things Paul exemplified what it means to be an authentic pastor. But men whose hearts have not been radically changed by the Holy Spirit will likely fall short in each one of these matters. They will preach and teach one or two doctrines to the exclusion of others, thinking they have discovered a panacea or wonder food.

But panaceas don't exist and nothing can substitute for a balanced variety of foods.

Counterfeit pastors are also likely to deliver strong warnings of doom and destruction—but they lack unction because these men hold themselves aloof from their hearers. They may sound the alarm—fire, fire!—but they are too busy to plan fire drills or to help conduct an orderly evacuation of the burning building. Instead they seem intent on creating havoc.

What frequently lies beneath this compulsion to raise the alarm is a desire to be noticed which can often be linked with the covetousness that is idolatry (Col. 3:5). The only difference between those who seek notoriety and those who seek money is that the former tend to preach alarming messages which anger the more affluent members of their congregations.

According to some of these prophets, California will fall into the sea, Henry Kissinger is the antichrist, and J. Edgar Hoover was a communist agent. Famines, floods and earthquakes spice their proclamations plentifully. But such things serve no useful end. The sheep grow restless, but not in such a way as to bring them more fully into the life of Christ. Most of these things do not really touch their lives in any real sense. They are sensational and titillating, but not life changing.

How Undershepherds Guard the Door

Jesus makes sure that the pastor-shepherds come in legitimately, and, in turn, He asks them to stand with Him at the door to insure that only sheep are admitted to the fold. The two-fold function of the door is aptly summarized in the *Broadman Bible Commentary* (John 10):

> In v. 8 Jesus regulates the access of shepherds to the sheep, whereas in v. 9 he regulates the access of the sheep to fold and pasture. In other words, Christ alone controls both the ministry and the membership of the church. Whereas the rulers of the old Israel were

> accredited by hereditary (priests, kings) and by human ordination (rabbis), the leaders of the new Israel were admitted to service only by Christ. Likewise, whereas one gained entry to the old Israel by circumcision, sacrifice, and faithfulness to the Law, one may enter the new Israel BY ME, i.e., through personal faith in Christ. (vol. 9, p. 305)

Becoming a part of the flock of God is the greatest thing that can ever happen to us. It is no wonder that many try to get in who are not sheep. But it is my responsibility as a pastor-shepherd to stand with Jesus at the door to prevent those who would come in under false pretense. No one can make himself a sheep; God must change him. I must look people over to find out whether they have experienced this supernatural work of regeneration. If not, I must do my best to lead them to Christ. I must keep them out of membership until they have become a genuine sheep.

When cattle or sheep are transported across state or national boundaries, they must be inspected for disease. Often they are quarantined for a time to insure that all danger of contagion is past. It is not enough to take the owner's word that these sheep are healthy; the officials run their own tests.

When someone comes to me from another local church, a letter from their previous pastor is essential, but it is not enough. I will also conduct my own tests.

Catechism Sorts the Sheep

In a work as large as ours, I cannot know each and every new person immediately. So, before anyone is permitted to become an active member of this local church, he must submit to nine months of basic Bible doctrine, which we call "Catechism One." All of the fundamentals of salvation are covered by means of questions and answers. We don't aim only at head knowledge, but at a genuine heart-changing experience in each person.

Instructors and counselors check the people to make sure they participate in each phase of salvation: repentance, faith, water baptism, the baptism in the Holy Spirit. They counsel with the people and try to sense their inner attitudes. Are they teachable and submissive? How do they feel when truth runs counter to their opinions and life styles?

The length of time required for this—nine months—eliminates those who are merely curious and who are otherwise not seriously committed. But the genuinely hungry become enthusiastically involved.

Completion of catechism entitles a person to be confirmed in the faith by the local presbytery (elders) who lay their hands upon them. But even this is not membership. Confirmation is a strengthening of a person in the faith and a sealing of the truths taught in catechism. It prepares us for the tests of faith that will surely come. Confirmation roots us in Christ rather than in a particular congregation. We see this in the work of the Apostles Paul and Barnabas. "And when they had preached the gospel to that city, and had taught many, they returned again to Lystra, and to Iconium, and Antioch, confirming the souls of the disciples, and exhorting them to continue in the faith, and that we must through much tribulation enter into the kingdom of God" (Acts 14:21-22).

A further step, however, is required before anyone can become a member. We are a community of tithers. We all share the responsibility of building and maintaining God's property over which we are stewards. No one can become one of us unless he promises to tithe both his money and his time. In addition to that he must agree to conform to our standards of conduct and dress. Each person becomes a contributor in one way or another. There are no useless members; every one has an important function, even if it is a hidden one.

Sometimes people get offended by such demands. I remember well a certain gentleman who wanted to become a member of the

Bethesda Missionary Temple. I described some of our procedures. He would have to attend catechism, find the Lord as Savior, be buried with Christ in baptism, receive the seal of the Spirit, become a tither, and submit himself to church doctrine and discipline for personal behavior.

When I finished, his neck and face were red. "I can join any church I want to in the city of Detroit. I don't have to go through this rigamarole. I like your church, but I am not going through all of that."

I agreed that there were other churches he could join more easily. I urged him to shop around and find one. He would not become my enemy for doing it. And I told him to let me know if ever I could be of further service to him.

He was furious as he walked out of my study. There was no reason why I should expect him back again.

But, a few months later, I received a phone call from him. We met in my office a few days later. He told me that he had indeed done some shopping around and he realized that the churches he could join were not worth joining. Anybody could get in. There was no inspection.

So he asked my forgiveness, enrolled himself in our catechism class, and became a member in Bethesda where he continues to this day.

To lower these standards would make people think they are sheep of God's pasture when they are not. Instead, God uses these standards to help people submit to the process the Bible calls conversion.

On the day of Pentecost the apostles stood by the door of the sheepfold with Christ. After Peter had preached the word of the Lord with convicting power and the people asked what to do, Peter, and the others with him, had a sure word of instruction: "Repent, and be baptized every one of you in the name of Jesus Christ for the remission of sins, and ye shall receive the gift of the

Holy Ghost'' (Acts 2:38).

This way is the only way—the legitimate door—into the sheepfold. Submission to Christ meant obedience to His undershepherds. If people will not submit to the admission requirements at the door, they will not submit to church government once inside.

CHAPTER 8

The Sheepfold as It Ought to Be

In our day there is considerable discussion about the true nature of the sheepfold—the local church. Some insist that this means the church of a given vicinity—the church in Detroit, in Seattle, in Philadelphia, etc., because in the ancient Near East one large sheepfold served each area and it was usually in the largest city or town of the district. This one fold housed many flocks, each with its own shepherd. That may have been true for the countryside, but certainly not for a city the size of Jerusalem. This interpretation is based largely on John 10:16, "And other sheep I have, which are not of this fold: them also I must bring, and they shall hear my voice; and there shall be one fold, and one shepherd."

But there Jesus is talking about the breaking down of the distinctions between the Jew and the Gentile. Once the sheep come in through Him as the Door, they lose their national and ethnic distinctions and become one. Jesus' emphasis is upon there being only one Shepherd—himself. Unity is created as all the sheep, regardless of previous background, relate to Him.

Many people tend to think of the sheepfold only in terms of the large yard in which sheep are kept near the marketplace. A.W. Pink describes this type of fold:

> In Palestine, which in the pastoral sections was infested with wild beasts, there was in each village a large sheepfold, which was the common property of the native farmers. This sheepfold was protected by a wall some ten or twelve feet high. When night fell, a number of different shepherds would lead their flocks up to the door of the fold, through which they passed, leaving them in the care of the porter, while they went home or sought lodging. At the door, the porter lay on guard through the night, ready to protect the sheep against thieves and robbers, or against wild animals which might scale the walls. In the morning the different shepherds returned. The porter would allow each one to enter through the door, calling by name the sheep which belonged to his flock. The sheep would respond to his voice, and he would lead them out to pasture. (*Exposition of the Gospel of John,* pp. 102-103)

But this was not the only kind of sheepfold. Sheep were often pastured far from the centers of population. In that event each shepherd built his own enclosure. Some of these were elaborate with high walls and even a tower. Others were hastily thrown together by weaving bramble bushes, or by setting a small stone wall in front of the mouth of a cave.

These folds answer to the churches in various communities. Pastor-shepherds are responsible to build enclosures for the sheep as well as to lead them.

Some time ago it was my pleasure to journey through Australia and New Zealand on a preaching and teaching tour. Some years prior to my visit, other preachers had gone through the land teaching an anti-building philosophy. Their arguments were:

(1) The money should be spent on people and not on buildings.

(2) People have a tendency to worship buildings.

(3) Buildings produce spiritual pride that should be avoided.

But God created man with the innate desire to build. God is a builder and creator. Jesus said, "I will build my church and the gates of hell shall not prevail against it." And Christ is building His church with embellishments which will make it glorious and beautiful (Eph. 5:27).

Our church buildings should be adequate and comfortable. A building usually reflects the kind of people who occupy or use it. You will know the kind of people Ann and I are by the kind of home we live in and how we decorate and maintain it.

When I see a church building unpainted, run down at the heels, its yard unmowed, and rest rooms cleaned by somebody who threw a sponge at the door, I know what kind of congregation I will meet.

People build buildings that reflect their feelings about themselves. In Washington, D.C., our government has erected buildings which speak of the glory and the grandeur of this nation. The physical decay of our cities says a lot about us too. We no longer build and maintain magnificent libraries, art institutes, symphony and concert halls. Today a domed football stadium is much more important than a symphony hall. This speaks volumes about the kind of people we have become and the culture we presently embrace. Should the body of Christ follow suit? Are the walls of our buildings to be barren of art, sculpture, and other things of beauty? I don't think so.

This is one reason why I have discouraged the church-in-the-home concept. It does not meet the deep human need to belong to something of value and significance.

The Sheepfold Speaks of Home

Hebrew, not surprisingly, is rich in words which describe the sheepfold. It will help us break the stereotypes if we examine these different words.

The most common Hebrew term, *navah*, means, in its various forms as both a noun and a verb, an abode of shepherds or flocks, a habitation (poetic), a meadow, to dwell or abide, a pasture. It connotes a feeling of peace because we know we belong. This term may be applied to simple sheepfolds, such as caves, or it may apply to the more elaborate structures. What is important here is that the sheep are at home.

Travel is usually enjoyable. But it's no fun without a place to call home. Vacations are refreshing because we have a home to which we can return.

King Solomon used *navah* in his prayer of sanctification of the temple (2 Chron. 6:40-42). Here it denotes God's resting place.

The Jerusalem temple at that time was uniquely the resting place of God. God has always been everywhere at once, but he designated specific places at different times to reveal His presence to the people. Thus He showed himself in the fiery pillar and cloud as Israel journeyed through the Sinai wilderness. Later He dwelt between the cherubim on the ark of the covenant. This same ark was transferred from the tabernacle of Moses into Solomon's temple. Then one day God became flesh and dwelt among us in the person of Jesus of Nazareth. At Pentecost He came to indwell each believer in the person of the Holy Spirit. This He continues to do. And beyond this, in a most special and beautiful way, He comes into the local church when we gather together to worship. Paul states that we are ". . . the building fitly framed together [that] groweth unto an holy temple in the Lord: In whom ye also are builded together for an habitation of God through the Spirit" (Eph. 2:21-22).

God now has a home—a resting place—among His praising people. It was not long after the end of World War II that our church began to discover new dimensions of fellowship and worship when it dawned on us that the local church was to be "a habitation—a home for God in the Spirit." We learned that God builds a temple out of our corporate worship and that Christ sings with His people when they assemble in His name (Heb. 2:12).

Today some seem to have shifted the emphasis from worship to discipling and teaching. They have taken away the fun of being one of God's sheep. Continual intensive study and teaching without the joy of worship will produce spiritual eggheads who know little or nothing about real living. The local church is a place where we should be at home in God's presence and enjoy the beauty of worship.

When groups splinter from the congregation, they become problem-oriented. Instead of centering on worship and the word, they are taken up with mechanics and structure. The local church is to be the place where God's presence rests among His people while they worship together. And it is there that we find rich pasture through the preaching of the word. We need to strike a balance between these two: worship and teaching.

The Sheepfold Protects

Sheep need protection from robbers, wild animals, and adverse weather. In some places these dangers are greater than in others. At times a cave or a hastily formed enclosure of thorn bushes was all that was needed. But in certain areas, known to be infested with Bedouin tribes which preyed upon the shepherds pasturing their flocks far from civilization, strong structures were needed, with towers to help the shepherds see danger from afar and prepare for it (2 Chron. 26:9-10; Mic. 4:8, etc.).

But strong fortifications were not enough. The walls needed watching. Thomson, describing present-day sheepfolds in Lebanon, says:

> Those low, flat buildings out on the sheltered side of the valley are sheepfolds . . . when the nights are cold, the flocks are shut up in them, but in ordinary weather they are merely kept within the yard. This, you observe, is defended by a wide stone wall, crowned all around with sharp thorns, which the prowling wolf will rarely attempt to scale . . . the leopard and panther of this country—when pressed with hunger, will overleap this thorny hedge, and with one tremendous bound land among the frightened fold. Then is the time to try the

> nerve and heart of a faithful shepherd. . . . As spring advances, they will move higher up to other marahs and greener ranges; and in the hot months of summer they sleep with their flocks on the cool heights of the mountains, with no other protection than a stout palisade of tangled thorn-bushes. (*The Land and the Book,* pp. 201-202)

The sheep usually remain outside the sheepfold with a shepherd watching over them (Gen. 31:39; Luke 2:8, etc.). By instinct the sheep will huddle together, hoping for safety in numbers. But real protection must come from the shepherd and his dogs. The shepherd defends the sheep with weapons: the sling, the rod, a gun. Like David, he must personally contend with the intruder, whether it be a lion, or bear, or a band of robbers. It is when this human hedge is broken down through neglect, laziness, or lack of interest that the sheep are endangered.

Pastor-shepherds can become dispirited, and, periodically, every pastor-shepherd must be renewed in pastoral concern and oversight.

Protecting the sheep means more than love and emotional concern. It also means an outward stance of vigilance against enemies. Sheep are exploited easily by those who twist the Scriptures to their own advantage. This means that pastor-shepherds must be able to distinguish subtle errors and so feed their sheep that they will not be easily enticed into by-paths. Paul protected the Ephesians by refusing to shrink from declaring to them the whole counsel of God. He urged the elders to take heed of the flock in which the Holy Spirit had made them guardians by feeding the church of the Lord. This would provide the surest protection against wolves from without and false teachers from within. Prevention was preferable to cure.

Some years back, a group of ministers whom I knew well fell into the trap of believing that the grace of God was license. One of them supposedly received a revelation from God based on Romans

8:10: "And if Christ be in you, the body is dead because of sin; but the Spirit is life because of righteousness." This meant to him that if a person was in Christ, the body was dead in the sight of the Lord and whatever the body did was of no consequence. This opened the way for drunkenness, adultery, homosexuality, and what have you.

When I heard what they were teaching, I confronted some of the men. But they were evasive. Some weeks later I received a visit from one of the men whom I had known for years. He asked me if he could conduct a series of meetings at Bethesda.

I answered, "Not until we have a few things straight." Shortly, and to my horror, I learned that all I had heard was true. I denied him the meeting, refused to bid him God speed, and made it clear that neither he nor any of his friends would be welcome in the church or in the homes of any of the flock.

The Sheepfold Restrains the Sheep

The Hebrew word, *miklah*, also means an enclosure or fold. It derives from a verb, *kala,* meaning to shut up, or withhold. This may seem to contradict Jesus' description of the sheepfold as a place we would go in and out of to find pasture, but it is not. Bill Gothard has aptly summarized liberty as the power to do what we should, rather than the license to do as we please.

God apparently made sheep to be domesticated by men. Wild sheep do not have highly developed wool. They have brown coats with an undercoat of wool only during the wintertime. The fine wool we find so valuable for felting and weaving today is the result of controlled crossbreeding supervised by men. As the sheep of God's pasture we are not valuable until we find our place in a local church and submit to the pastor-shepherd.

We have trained a number of men at Bethesda to be pastors. Two of them especially come to mind. Both had been in religious settings with little or no discipline. In time they had come to realize their potential was unharnessed and dissipating. They came to

Bethesda and submitted themselves to its leadership and training. There they methodically handled the word of God, led in prayer, and performed some seemingly menial tasks. They submitted and did each of their jobs well. Under this discipline, the charisma of the Holy Spirit took on evident proportions. The sheep were responding to them, liking them, seeking them out.

When, in God's time, they were ready to lead their own flocks, the sheep felt secure with them. They had proved they were not fly-by-nights and, when situations arose for which they were unprepared, they maintained close fellowship and harmony with our church in Detroit. Looking back, I do not believe that either of these men would have made it if they had not submitted themselves to discipline so that their wool could be domesticated.

Wild sheep are not so free as we might at first suppose. To be sure, they are more rugged and versatile, and less helpless, than domesticated sheep. But they can never achieve the intelligence and resourcefulness of the man who shepherds. Thus, when cold or famine or drought make living hard, the wild sheep perish in proportionately larger numbers than do their domesticated cousins. In the same way, Christians who hold themselves aloof from the authority of the church place themselves in a dangerous position. God's sheep are limited in what they can glean from the Bible. Sheep need to be taught by qualified pastor-shepherds.

When sheep are allowed to go unchecked along the paths of least resistance, they do not grow. Instead, they become slaves to habit. Only external restraint can lift sheep above the pull of their natural tendencies and build into them the character God intends.

In the confinement of the sheepfold, each sheep finds its place. But don't think of this sheepfold as a small pen or courtyard. The prophet Micah talked of order in the spiritual remnant of Israel in terms of the abundant flocks of Bozrah (2:12-13). Order and discipline do not necessarily require a small group. We must remember that God consistently called the entire nation of Israel His flock and at the time of the exodus this meant at least two million people. What brought about the order, the discipline, and the safety, was the careful shepherding by their leader, Moses, and his assistants. Whatever the size of the flock, its order, discipline, and safety depend upon the skill and faithfulness of the pastor-shepherd. He alone can bring the wayward, wandering sheep into a meaningful community of mutual commitment:

> Shepherd thy people with thy staff,
> the flock of thy inheritance,
> who dwell alone in a forest
> in the midst of a garden land;
> let them feed in Bashan and Gilead
> as in the days of old.
>
> Micah 7:14 RSV

CHAPTER 9

Feed the Flock of God

We turn now from the matter of shelter to the matter of food. No shepherd will have his flock long if he cannot feed them adequately. And the size of his flock depends largely upon the amount of pasture he has at his disposal and the accessibility of water. Not long ago a friend of mine who pastors in Virginia experienced a wonderful visitation of God. The services of the church were consistently crowded; young people, especially, were traveling to them from all over the area.

Finally, some of his fellow pastors in that vicinity called him to protest and ask questions. They had worked long and hard to provide the best in music and other things that might attract young people, but with few results. What was he doing that was drawing the kids in such unprecedented numbers? "I don't know," my friend replied. "I guess we just feed them."

Sheep Need Fresh Pastures

We think of feeding in terms of putting the bottle or the spoon to the baby's mouth and encouraging him to swallow. But this is not what the Bible means by feeding sheep. The Hebrew word *ra'ah* means "to provide pasture and allow sheep to graze." The shepherd has only to lead the way to grass and the sheep will do their own eating. And he must keep the flock moving regularly lest they overgraze a given area. We pastors likewise cannot endlessly repeat the same portions of Scripture or specialize in a few doctrines. We must proclaim the full counsel of God. We must provide balanced teaching.

The Millers, in their *Encyclopedia of Bible Life* describe the feeding work of the Oriental shepherd in this way:

> [The shepherd] . . . knew "the green pastures," every one of them, below the terraced farms of Bethlehem. He knew how to walk at the head of the sheep group, *leading* them—not following them as western shepherds do—to the rest beside "the still waters." He stayed away from the torrential streams rushing to join the Nimrin, the Jordan, or the Orontes River, or the sea. The still waters known to the Psalmist were the wells, pools, and quiet rivulets or sheltered sand bars, such as we see where the Dog River enters the Mediterranean in summer. There, under a bridge we have never failed to see drinking flocks, watched by resting shepherds who have led them from Syrian highlands. The "paths of righteousness" were age-old sheep-walks used since the beginnings of the Hebrew people. (p. 34)

Part of feeding the sheep is providing a restful atmosphere for eating and digesting. Sheep are restless as long as they are hungry or whenever they sense or imagine danger. They will not lie down unless they feel secure. And the presence of the shepherd reassures them more than anything. He shows them the best food and protects them from enemies.

Feeding the flock is a little like raising a family. You have to set a variety of nutritious foods before them and dissuade them from eating too much junk food. Some of the sheep in my flock would prefer that I spend more time talking about healing than I do; others wish I'd stay more with apocalyptic subjects like the mark of the beast and the identity of the beast's seven heads and ten horns. Still others tell me they want to hear about nothing except the gifts of the Spirit. Then there are those who can't get enough of gospel quartet music—and those who become ill at the mention of quartets.

Needless to say, feeding a congregation will involve conflict—tears, frustration, disappointment. But unless they're fed properly they'll become weak and ill. In the long run, well-nourished sheep will be contented sheep. And there will be time for a hot fudge sundae now and then.

Another factor determines how much and what kinds of food a flock will eat: seasonal differences. Sometimes pastures are plentiful and rich; at other times they may be sparse and hard to find. Occasionally, when pastures are altogether unavailable, the shepherd must forage on behalf of his flock just to keep them alive. Thomson stresses that such times are the exception rather than the rule:

> In ordinary circumstances the shepherd does not *feed* his flock, except by leading and guiding them where they may gather for themselves; but there are times when it is otherwise. Late in autumn, when the pastures are dried up, and in winter, in places covered with snow, he must furnish them with food, or they die. In the vast oak woods along the eastern sides of Lebanon, between Baalbek and the cedars, there are then gathered innumerable flocks, and the shepherds are all day long in the bushy trees, cutting down the branches, upon whose leaves and tender twigs the sheep and goats are entirely supported. The same is true in all mountain districts, and large forests are preserved on purpose. (*The Land and the Book*, p. 204)

In the *Encyclopaedia Britannica* we read:

> It is seldom profitable to feed grain to breeding sheep or sucking lambs as long as they have an abundance of succulent grazing forage. Though they do best on

> pastures and ranges which provide choice grass or legume forage which is short and fine, they will consume considerable quantities of high, coarse, bushy material and weeds. Hay and other roughage can be used, particularly in winter or drought periods. Grain may be used in small amounts for flushing at breeding times and, of course, for fattening. (vol. 20, p. 364)

Thus, during ordinary conditions, the pastor-shepherd opens to his flock highland pastures of the Bible under the guidance of the Spirit. He also depends on the Holy Spirit to help each believer to feed upon what he needs. There are truths which we "need that no man teach us" (1 John 2:27). But we don't ordinarily go where we don't want to go. The pastor-shepherd must urge us into those portions of God's word that will change us as we obey them. We need wisdom to maintain that delicate balance wherein we exercise our pastoral authority boldly but without diminishing the individual believer's direct relationship with God.

I meet with the adult teachers of our church once a month to go over the lessons we have written for their use. I discuss the highlights of the lesson and explain whatever particulars are not self-evident. The lessons themselves give the teachers a great deal of information which they can ingest and digest during each week. Most of them have neither the time nor the background to provide this grazing land for themselves. But as they are thus shepherded to green pastures, they in turn can lead their Bible class students to similarly verdant feeding places on Sunday.

God did not intend for pastoral authority to conflict with each believer's access to God (each believer's priesthood), but to work together. In the New Testament we find that both things are fully inculcated without any sense of contradiction. Take, for example, the two following passages, both from the pen of the same author:

> . . . I will put my laws into their mind, and write them in their hearts: and I will be to them a God, and they shall be to me a people: And they shall not teach every man his

> brother, saying, Know the Lord: for all shall know me, from the least to the greatest. (Heb. 8:10-11)
>
> . . . be . . . followers of them who through faith and patience inherit the promises. (Heb. 6:12)

They don't contradict but they do create tension. We hate tension and are generally more comfortable without it. Thus church history is a record of pendulum swings from authoritarianism to libertarianism. We want either to sit by comfortably while someone else takes all the responsibility off our shoulders, or we want to do our own thing without any restraints. But God thwarts our desires at both ends of the pendulum's swing. He ordained the tension between authority and liberty and it is in that tension that we will most fully experience His life.

Our leaders should bring us to good pastures and protect us from our enemies. But we are supposed to eat as the Holy Spirit makes the Scriptures personally alive to us. We need to hear God's voice both through undershepherds and through reading the Bible. If we become deaf to either of these sources, we tend to lose our way.

> There is one body, and one Spirit, even as ye are called in one hope of your calling; One Lord, one faith, one baptism, One God and Father of all, who is above all, and through all, and in you all. (Eph. 4:4-6)

Each of us directly encounters God, but we are drawn together through various means because God chooses them for our good. In the succeeding verses Paul talks of apostles, prophets, evangelists, pastors and teachers who help the saints for the work of the ministry to build up the body of Christ. Without these God-ordained men and women performing their tasks in the church, people will not become all they were meant to be.

The Bible often presents truth in terms of a paradox. Periodically the Holy Spirit may call our attention to some aspect of truth, as He is in these days stirring us regarding leadership in the care of God's people. But the other part of the paradox—the priesthood of every believer—is there for the purpose of balance.

As we step forward on the right foot, we must soon put our weight on the left.

For some time a group of more than forty people had been meeting in a small town in Florida. A pastor-shepherd from a hundred miles away met with them on Friday evenings once a week. Each week the people would flock around him and besiege him with questions and problems. They begged him to begin regular catechism studies.

"No," he replied with sincere regret. "I don't believe that is my privilege. This should wait until your pastor comes. I believe God is preparing one for you, and you should be praying for him." This man understood something basic. Whoever brought these people into vital contact with the Lord through the teaching of catechism would also be gathering them as sheep around himself. This man did not want to build a relationship with these people he could not maintain. Nor did he want to make it harder for their real pastor to draw the sheep around him.

Months passed while people in Florida and in Detroit prayed for someone to hear God's call to feed these hungry people. In time, a couple responded and went to look over the situation. I urged them to be cautious because I didn't want them to sell out here and move down there for a transient situation.

Before they came, the man who had been teaching the fledgling flock had prayed, "Lord, when your man comes, as a sign to me, let all the people who flock around me every Friday night gather around him instead—even down to the last child." As he listened to the man's sermon, God gently whispered to him, "This is the pastor." Still, he waited for the response of the sheep.

After the service, they all gathered for refreshments. The children had baked cookies for this great event. As usual, the people began to crowd in on all sides with their questions and problems. But then something happened. Conversation began to grow up around the guest speaker and his wife. Soon their table was crowded. People were standing three-deep to hear what they had to say. Before long, the Friday night pastor-shepherd was left alone with his wife. Every one of the sheep—even to the last child—had gathered around their new pastor. God had answered prayer.

Thus assured that the right person had come to assume the full responsibility of the work, he later spoke frankly with the incoming pastor-shepherd, "I have told these people that once their pastor came, I did not want them to call me any more. The sheep should come to you with all of their needs. We can meet together for prayer, for talking things over, or just for fun in order to relieve pressure. But the sheep are yours from here on out. They must rely upon you for their food."

CHAPTER 10

We Are the Community

Sheep have relationships with one another as well as with their pastor. They have something in common. They enjoy the same care. They eat the same food. They feel at home with each other. This is what community is all about. God has created all His animals with a built-in need to be together.

This need to herd is one of the most basic motivations of animal and human behavior. We consider it normal to seek community and abnormal to shy away from it.

> Nature's creatures often exhibit impulses of self-assertion and competition. But all through life's vast range, these instincts are balanced by another kind of drive. Nature does not implant in her children the simple message: "Take care of yourself." Ancient and universal, there is a second injunction: "Get together." It is as vital as the breath of life. Every creature has a need for companionship as biologically important as food and drink. Testing tadpoles, zoologists have found that even these humble creatures are so deeply influenced by social need that a solitary tadpole can regenerate an injured part of its body only slowly, but if

> it is given the dimly sensed companionship of fellow tadpoles its healing powers speed up almost miraculously. (Reader's Digest [editors] *Our Amazing World of Nature: Its Marvels,* p. 20)

We were not designed to be at our best alone. Birds of a feather do flock together. Sheep herd. Cattle herd. Everybody gets together. Nobody wants to be isolated. This should make it the natural thing to gather sheep in our churches. If we are not able to capitalize on this herding instinct, then we are going against the grain in some way. It is unnatural to repel people.

To go with the grain is much like sliding down a banister. But, if you go against the grain, you will get splinters. Some people seem to be going against the grain all the time. They get consequences instead of results.

The Holy Spirit adds a dimension to our natural instinct to gather in groups. Those who have made the sheep of God's pasture through redemption feel a special affinity for each other. The Holy Spirit draws people together by shedding His love abroad in our hearts.

The world is falling apart at the seams. In cities like Detroit there has been a total breakdown of community. When we were kids growing up, we had neighborhood communities. We were "the Beall kids." We were the family who lived in the middle of the block. Everybody in the community knew Mr. and Mrs. Beall and their children.

If we started tearing up anybody's property, people knew what to do. They went to our parents who took us in hand and taught us to become creative and useful. The community was important to us as we grew up. We had community baseball teams. We belonged, and that belonging gave us a sense of identity. We knew where we had roots and we knew that we mattered to those around us.

But in our complicated urban society, people get a feeling of anonymity, not identity. Our church in Detroit is not a community church. We draw from the total metropolitan area, as much as sixty and eighty miles away.

But, even though we don't serve a community or parish, the Holy Spirit works among us to build a community, not based upon geography, but in Him. How have we developed this deep sense of belonging to one another? We teach the sheep to appreciate one another. By word and example, we show the people how to care for one another.

The early church began in local units based on earthly concepts of community. But after a while the church itself became a community—a spiritual community. It was not the city that mattered now, but mutual ties to Jesus Christ. As John put it: "That which we have seen and heard declare we unto you, that ye also may have fellowship with us: and truly our fellowship is with the Father, and with his Son Jesus Christ" (1 John 1:3).

Until our relationship with God is established through redemption, the basis for our human relationships will be fragile and inadequate. *Koinonia* is not only sharing, but a joint participation in something bigger than ourselves.

Because Christian community is based in God and not, ultimately, in human concerns, its values are quite different than those of the social order out of which the church draws its members. The old social order is built on idolatry which proclaims the supremacy of man and his desires. But the new order is built on the reign of God, whose ways are not our ways. Jesus said the reign of God was like a little leaven that leavens the whole lump. Among other things, that means that wherever the church exists —wherever men and women worship and obey Christ—the surrounding social order will be inexorably affected. It is seldom, if ever, dramatic or sudden. Like leaven it works silently, slowly and relentlessly.

The social order of ancient Greco-Roman civilization was divided between slaves and free men. And women, even if they were free, were accorded a status only slightly better than the slaves. But the reign of God slowly erased these noxious distinctions (Gal. 3:28). Christ gives positive identity to His servants who therefore need no longer find their identity in being a Jew or a woman or a slave. What they had in common in the Lord came to mean more than natural differences and social distinctions.

Because the church is ahead of the social order, there is always a certain tension between the two. If we adjust our behavior to that which the Bible demands, we will not be able to conform to the outside world at the same time. We can only fit one mold at a time. The more important the new community of the Spirit becomes to us the less we will be fashioned according to outside standards. We will dress and behave according to the group that matters the most to us. Community pressure helps us to sever our relations with the world system and to follow after Christ. In the community we find ourselves able to change in practical ways that which would seem very difficult if we attempted them alone.

We rise from the waters of baptism to walk in newness of life, but not automatically. Habits must be relearned. Unless we embrace new community values and decide that our identity among the redeemed matters more than the world's opinion, even outward behavioral change will only come slowly.

Basic Human Needs

We enter into a whole new realm through a second birth (John 3:3, 5). Just as in natural birth, we are born into the kingdom of God with many basic needs which must be supplied through others. These needs are not only spiritual, but emotional, intellectual, and physical as well. We are moving from one social order to another; all our thinking and values are being changed. The church gives to us spiritually, and meets our deep psychological needs as well. Otherwise we could not be weaned from the world's social order. The new community must be able to supply every kind of need that was formerly met in the outside social order.

The Need to Belong

We have to see our name somewhere. If we cannot do it any other way, we will sign up for a gasoline card at the gas station. We may not even use the credit cards once we have them, but we are a part of something.

People must know whether or not they belong to our churches. Joining must be a significant event—one that makes a lasting impression. It is too casual if we tell everyone who wants to be a member to come up front on a particular Sunday morning and shake our hands. If the church is going to meet this human need to belong, becoming a part of our community must be important.

I've already outlined the procedure through which a person must pass to become a member of Bethesda Missionary Temple. It usually takes a year from the time a person initially decides he wants to become a member until he is formally welcomed by the pastors and elders into that position. Needless to say the occasion of this welcoming is far from casual. We trust it is not ostentatious, but it is an event of some moment in our congregation. And it leaves no doubt in the minds of those who have undergone it: they belong.

The Need for Significance

The community to which we belong must make us special in some way. This is only possible when the community itself receives recognition on a wide scale. Denominational religion is strong when it comes to this. When you are in a social gathering and the subject of religion comes up, those who belong to major denominations have a real advantage. Someone asks, "What religion are you?"

A fellow squares his shoulders and answers, "I'm a Lutheran."

Another proudly says, "I'm a Catholic."

The next person declares, "I'm Presbyterian."

These are all labels that carry a lot of weight. But when they ask us independents, "What are you?" we have quite a job of explaining on our hands.

It is a tremendous psychological blow to recognize that we belong to something that has no significance in the social order. Those of us who pastor independent churches must labor at this point, especially for our young people. This matter of significance and identity really devastates kids in high school.

When I went to high school we had a good church name, but the problem was that my mother was the minister. I didn't want anybody to know that because I couldn't explain it.

Somebody would come up to me and say, "Hey, Beall, I hear your mother's the preacher! What kind of a church do you have?"

I'd say, "I don't ask you about your religion, so don't ask me about mine."

No adolescent wants to be regarded as weird or freakish, and, on points like this one, the pressure of the old social order to conform to its accepted standards can be overwhelming. What did it signify that I belonged to an independent church of which my mother was the minister? Did it mean I was odd, out of order? Yes, in one sense, it did. The old order hadn't yet recognized and adjusted to this new sign of the kingdom of God. Today independents are more widely recognized and even the Episcopal church has decided to ordain women to the priesthood. But living in the community that God creates will inevitably challenge our need for significance. It will be met as we gain the strength to repudiate the implication that we are inherently strange and, with the help of the Holy Spirit, feel good about being Christians who stand independent of traditional denominations.

The same holds true concerning spiritual gifts. To think that the only significant contributions people can make to the church are in the area of the nine spiritual gifts is a serious mistake. The gifts of the Spirit must never be minimized, but neither should they eclipse everything else. For one thing, many people do not know what their spiritual gifts are or how to exercise them. If we put a premium on them, these people don't feel they are contributing to the community.

At Bethesda we once experienced a period that nearly devastated us because we did not know how to help people find their best way of contributing. God was showing us that by laying our hands on people and prophesying over them, they could be established in places of usefulness in the body of Christ. But in our excitement, we temporarily lost our balance. People in the church almost stopped doing things entirely because they had not experienced the laying on of hands and a direct revelation from God about their calling. They were feeling, without anything being said, that their contribution was not really worthwhile until it had been confirmed by the presbytery. So they stopped what they were doing to wait for a word of direction through others. And those who did receive the laying on of hands generally would not contribute beyond the realms specified by the prophecy spoken over them. We had a church full of people who were in turmoil about their area of contribution.

During another time the most important work in our church seemed to be teaching. If you were not a teacher, you just were not optimally important or vital to the work. Singing in the choir, for example, was not nearly so prestigious as teaching. Consequently, we had a problem getting people to usher, to sing in the choir, or to serve on administrative committees.

The solution, we reasoned, lay not in demeaning teaching but in promoting other services. My brother Harry discovered ways to make the choir an outstanding place of contribution. He worked the choir members hard preparing for one musical presentation after another. The church was packed out for these concerts. Many people who never came through our doors on any other occasion attended them. He developed lighting, and costuming, and elaborate backdrops. Each cantata became a major happening. Now people are on the waiting list to join the choir.

We must develop many different avenues for contributing to the community. And each of these avenues must be accorded high esteem. If you come to Detroit, you will not only find those who are teachers of catechism, but you will find many working under them as counselors on a personal level. These counselors are an essential part of the catechism department. Not only do they grade the homework and keep attendance records, but they help students with personal problems. We have a waiting list of those who desire to be catechism counselors. Why? We have made it known that this is a vital area of contribution.

Other people make their contribution by getting materials ready for these classes. Still others set tables, prepare for social times with the children, make arrangements for confirmation services, maintain buildings, or take care of paperwork. But they are happy in what they are doing because we have made it known that everyone is needed. We appreciate the service of every single individual.

The Need for Approval

Another basic need of the human being is for approval. He must know not only that his contribution is important, but that he is making it to the satisfaction of those in authority over him. He needs commendation from time to time.

Regrettably, it is not always easy for those in leadership to supply this need. They may find themselves threatened by competence in those working under them and seek to hold them down in order to preserve their own positions.

In independent churches, the pastor-shepherd is all alone with the wind blowing against him and without a denomination standing behind him. He is the person who is going to see this church sink or swim. This situation creates a feeling of insecurity.

Without knowing it, the pastor-shepherd transfers this feeling of insecurity to his flock. Members of the flock in turn begin to compete with one another. Instead of welcoming competence and talent in others, they react defensively. People forget that they are on the same team and that when anyone scores, this is a victory for the whole local church. They are unable to rejoice when another is honored.

When the flock becomes anxious and insecure, they won't feed. The pastor-shepherd can be dishing out the greatest preaching in the world, but the sheep cannot digest it. We become restless and irritable. Whenever our basic needs are not being met, we cannot pasture properly. Before long, the sheep becomes faint. They start snapping at each other. The people don't know what ails them, but they lose their taste for the pasture and leave the flock.

We as leaders must give approval to those who work with us. If a person does something that is exemplary and good, we should tell them. But if we are unable to give approval because of our own insecurity, his need will not be met and he will develop problems. We must learn how to overcome our own insecurities and practice giving approval where it is merited.

These basic needs are not theoretical. They exist in the human personality. These social needs are as real as the drive for self-preservation or for sex. If the church community fails to meet them, the sheep will find satisfaction elsewhere. It is part of feeding the flock of God to make sure that our local community is coping with each one of these basic needs. This is the only way we can develop a contented and restful flock.

CHAPTER 11

Fighting over Water

Palestine is a semiarid land located on the southeastern corner of the Mediterranean where the sea and desert meet. Just as in Southern California, the moist air from the sea is blocked by mountains which confine most rain to the western slopes—to the east is true desert. Six months of the year are rainy; the other six months are dry. Summer is almost without rainfall. The earliest rains come in the fall and are eagerly awaited by farmers and shepherds alike. Rainfall is plentiful during the three months from early December to early March. Some snow may fall around Christmas. Then the rains taper off. A final time of heavy showers comes during April. This rain is crucial to the harvest. Since it comes at the end of the season, it is called the latter rain. It swells the grain, making it ready for harvest.

The latter rain is essential to the shepherd. It fills the cisterns for the beginning of summer. It also keeps the grass green a little longer.

According to the *Encyclopaedia Britannica*:

> Sheep need as much as 1½ gal. of water a day, though dew on grass or snow, if available, may suffice for much of the requirement. They should not have to travel more

> than three or four miles between grazing and water in cool weather, or about two miles in warm weather; animals with young should be even closer. Thus the number of animals which may be supported in a semiarid area is rather limited by the availability and spacing of water holes. (vol. 20, p. 364)

During the dry season, the shepherd must seek wells fed by underground springs. These are called wells of living water or waters that bubble up. Since their source is underground, they depend less directly on changing seasons or weather conditions. Cisterns, on the other hand, are mere storage places. They hold water that has come from the rains. This water supply is soon exhausted once the rainy season is past.

What does all of this have to do with the local church and God's sheep? In both the Old and New Testaments water is used as a figure of the Holy Spirit (John 4, Isa. 55), and wells speak of our capacity for God (John 4).

Water Is a Gathering Point

Sheep are watered each noon. The shepherds gather at the well or water hole. As long as there is plenty of water, this is a good time for the shepherds. They relax and refresh themselves as the sheep mingle. Listen to James Hastings' description of watering time:

> It is one of the most interesting spectacles to see a number of flocks of thirsty sheep brought by their shepherds to be watered at a fountain. Each flock, in obedience to the call of its own shepherd, lies down, awaiting its turn. The shepherd of one flock calls his sheep in squads, draws water for them, pours it into the troughs, and, when the squad has done, orders it away by sounds which the sheep perfectly understand, and calls up another squad. When the whole of one flock is watered, its shepherd signals to it, and the sheep rise, and move leisurely away, while another flock comes in a similar manner to the troughs, and so on, until all the

> flocks are watered. The sheep never make any mistake as to who whistles to them or calls them. (*A Dictionary of the Bible*, vol. IV, p. 487)

The shepherds become acquainted with one another during these watering times. And the sheep themselves also socialize. Just so, pastor-shepherds and their people must have times of refreshing in God's presence, when the Lord sovereignly showers His grace upon the services. Praise is easy and uplifting. People flood the altars. Needs are met.

We have found through the years that God singularly blesses our times of special convention each Easter and November. Why? I believe it is for several reasons:

(1) At convention time we extend ourselves to outsiders, even to the opening of our homes and the spending of hours of labor in the kitchen preparing meals, and the delight of eating together.

(2) We invite guest speakers and ministers—gifts to the body of Christ—who help the pastor-shepherds as well as the sheep.

(3) Everyone is encouraged to break from regular routine to wait upon God, to meet old and new friends, and to attend the stimulating services.

There is a prevailing atmosphere of excitement, anticipation, and openness. People are expecting God and He does not disappoint them. He often grants us fresh vision. The dreams and goals He gave us in the past are frequently restored to clearer focus. And, most especially, the truths God has been speaking to us for weeks and months are confirmed through two or three outside speakers who could only know what to say as God instructed them. New choruses are added to our repertoire and we discover additional avenues for thanking and praising God.

The conventions that have made a lasting impression upon us have one thing in common: a real flow of the Holy Spirit. Speakers did not collaborate on material and yet the messages dovetailed perfectly. Jesus Christ, the head of the church, was supplying necessary water and we were all refreshed.

Feuds Over Water Rights

Disputes regarding water rights were among the most common causes for war between shepherd families and tribes in the Middle East. Whoever dug a well and named it was its owner. But others often became jealous. People will do many things when they are competing for survival.

Enemies often deliberately plugged up wells. Isaac had to redig many wells in his day because the Philistines, envious of his wealth, had filled them with earth (Gen. 26:15). He had to endure contention and hatred before he found room in the land. This is often true in the ministry as well.

In the late forties and early fifties, the Lord sent a gracious refreshing upon many sections of the United States and Canada. Some called it "the latter rain," others "the move of God," while still others named it, "the healing revival." In fact, the choice of name usually reflected a person's previous denominational associations.

It was a joy to discover the new wells of blessing the Lord was opening up all over the land during this season of visitation. We would stand shoulder to shoulder with ministers and workers of every shade and hue, and drink of the water that flowed so abundantly. What fellowship! What singing! What love! But, in time, what contention!

Jealous and fearful pastor-shepherds began to insist that their flocks should be watered in one particular way only—their way.

Insignificant things began to divide us. Some men wanted to eliminate all hymnals. They argued that God was giving us new revelation. We must have new bottles for the new wine. Others rejoined that new songs were fine, but that each scribe instructed in the kingdom of God brings from his wares that new *and* the old (Matt. 13:52). They did not want to cut themselves off from the past.

The contention grew so hot around some wells over matters as insignificant as this, that all hands picked up sand and threw it into the well—sand of bitterness, strife and resentment.

Another way that we expressed our jealousy and competition was to give our wells—congregations—particular names or characteristics. Thus some of the churches specialized in praise, others in healing, still others in deliverance (exorcism). Particularly prominent among these motifs was prophecy. Sad to say, so much weight was placed on prophecy that its back was broken. People used it to pronounce doom, to usurp authority, and give vent to anger and rebellion. Lost was its capacity to edify and comfort.

Whichever motif a congregation selected, it was used as a means to elevate that group above all the others. A church that specialized in deliverance would hardly give the time of day to a brother who felt that praise was the be all and end all of the kingdom of God. A healing evangelist got a cold reception in churches that emphasized prophecy.

Thus the wells began to run dry and our joy was turned to sorrow. And we began to get thirsty, which is precisely what the Holy Spirit knew we needed. Thirsty people—needy people—are less likely to believe in their own self-sufficiency or to hold on to their jealousy. We learned to look at our true feelings about the successes of other pastors and churches, and about new ministers and congregations starting up in our vicinity. Then we could quickly confess our jealousy and be cleansed so that we could begin to dig wells and pray for rain for our entire region. In this way we have learned how to have plenty and still enjoy open fellowship with all our brethren.

And that's essential because we usually need to work together in order to get water for our flocks. Thomson's description of well covers will help us see why.

> I have frequently seen wells closed up with large stones . . . in the dreary deserts. Cisterns are very generally covered over with a large slab, having a round

> hole in it large enough to let down the leather bucket or earthen jar. Into this hole a heavy stone is thrust, often such as to require the united strength of two or three shepherds to remove. The same is true occasionally over wells of living water. But where they are large and the supply abundant no such precaution is needed. . . . I have repeatedly found wells closed up tight and the mouth plastered over with mortar. Such wells are reserved until times of greatest need, when all other sources of supply have failed. (*The Land the the Book*, p. 589)

The news media has been telling us for some time about the many churches that are folding. People have stopped attending these churches. The problem in every case is lack of water. The pastor-shepherds did not know how to welcome the work of the Holy Spirit. But those who have learned are enjoying exceptional growth. Sheep are being attracted from everywhere around these well-watered sheepfolds. In this day of charismatic visitation, many wells are being unstopped and many new ones dug. There is water enough for everyone if we will but put away fear and envy, and learn to embrace our brothers.

CHAPTER 12

Get Off Your Back!

When our basic needs are met and our vital organs function normally, we say that we are "in good health." The same is true of sheep. In manuals of animal husbandry, we find specific signs that are used as guidelines when the shepherds periodically check their sheep for wounds and disease.

(1) Healthy sheep look alert with a clear bold eye and with constantly pricked ears.
(2) Healthy sheep have good appetites.
(3) Healthy sheep walk with coordination, holding their heads and necks upright.
(4) Healthy sheep chew their cuds regularly. (We call this rumination.)
(5) Healthy sheep have a firm and unbroken fleece.
(6) Healthy sheep keep within the flock, except in mountain breeds which range scattered apart.
(7) Healthy sheep have sound feet.
(8) Healthy sheep have sound, unbroken teeth.

Shepherds check their sheep by picking them up and handling them and looking for evidences of pest infection, scabs, or listlessness. When they find something wrong, they apply the needed medication to eliminate pests. On occasion, it is necessary to run the sheep through a "sheep dip." Each night as the sheep return to the fold, the shepherd applies ointment to bruises and tears, and anoints the weary and overheated with cool, refreshing oil. Along with medication, the shepherd gives each sheep his tender affectionate care.

An experienced sheepman of Lebanon reveals this trade secret:

> The word 'shemen,' translated into English as 'oil,' really means Oriental butter, which is well-known in all the Orient by the similar Arabic word, 'semen,' and which all shepherds use as a remedy for their sick sheep. After admitting all his flock into the sheepfold, the shepherd cares for the sick sheep. He runs the 'shemen,' or butter, out of his horn and rubs their heads with it. If he is short of 'shemen,' he usually uses olive oil; sometimes he takes cedar tar out of his leather bag and applies it to the wounds and scratches which they have received; then with his brass cup, or 'tassy,' he gives them water to drink. (*The Shepherd Song on the Hills of Lebanon*, pp. 36, 112)

When sheep are healthy, all of their basic needs are met. Their life is balanced. They have the right food and water and exercise. The sum total of their condition is best expressed by the one word, 'contentment.' They are not distressed or 'diseased'; they are comfortable. They demonstrate their contentment by a playfulness which is almost like skipping or dancing.

> The mountains skipped like rams, and the little hills like lambs. (Psa. 114:4)

Manifestations of Discontent

Just as we can tell by watching the sheep's behavior whether or not he is healthy and content, so can we easily discern when he is not up to par. Discontent is noticeable. It is seen in the eyes, in the walk, and in gestures. When a sheep is not responding well and seems despondent, we say that it is a "cast" sheep. It is in need of the shepherd's work of restoration. It may have rolled over on its back and been unable to get up again. The shepherd may have to soothe it, massage it, and gradually lift it to its feet.

This common task of restoring "cast" sheep is what David was talking about when he extolled the Lord for "restoring his soul." Restoring the soul literally means "to be set on one's feet again."

Getting a person on his feet does not mean he has been unable to walk physically, but it means he has sat down emotionally and is needing someone to lift him. We call this sullen withdrawal into self-pity and discontent, "depression" or "melancholia." It means to be inwardly cast down—to be spiritually a "cast" sheep. Listen to Psalm 42:

> My tears have been my meat day and night, while they continually say unto me, Where is thy God? When I remember these things, I pour out my soul in me: for I had gone with the multitude, I went with them to the house of God, with the voice of joy and praise, with a multitude that kept holyday. Why are thou cast down, O my soul? and why art thou disquieted in me? hope thou in God: for I shall yet praise him for the help of his countenance. O my God, my soul is cast down within me. . . . (3-6)

God's people become cast just as natural sheep do—and, when they do, they need restoring. We can be honest as Christians and say when our souls need to be restored. We do not have to pretend or wear a mask.

Some people feel that we should go around with a false face and never admit anything is wrong. But they're wrong. We need to admit the way we feel, just as David did. That will open the door for genuine healing of the hurt that caused the anger which became depression because we didn't think it would do any good to express it.

David asked his soul why it was cast down. He worshiped daily at the temple. But on this certain day, life didn't seem rosy. Any of us can wake up to a day of depression. It could happen tomorrow morning. You could wake up and feel everything has gone wrong. When this happens, we need to ask why, as David did.

What is a disquieted soul? It is a soul that awakens to find its world turned upside down. We are nervous about the world. We don't know what ails us. We are anything but content! Peter writes about such feelings:

> . . . though now for a reason, if need be, ye are in heaviness through manifold temptations: That the trial of faith, being much more precious than of gold that perisheth, though it be tried with fire, might be found unto praise and honour and glory at the appearing of Jesus Christ. (1 Pet. 1:6-7)

It is necessary to our development that we pass through these times of heaviness. We are not always delivered speedily. Sometimes the heaviness continues for days. But it is only "for a season." We will come out of it.

God allows depression to teach each of us how to overcome it. He doesn't want us to become slaves to feelings and moods. We have a source of inner joy that comes from the spring and is not dependent on outward circumstances.

Stay Close to the Shepherd

Sheep become cast for a variety of reasons. The most common one is failure to pay attention to the shepherd. Sheep can become so involved in their pursuit of food that they fail to notice the shepherd's voice becoming distant. Preoccupied, they fail to notice that the flock has gone on. Others wander off because the shepherd is not sufficiently watchful. They find themselves far away from the flock and too weak to care for themselves. In their exhaustion and thirst, they carelessly lie down in a hollow. Their center of gravity shifts and they cannot get up again. Instead, their legs flail helplessly in the air. They bleat frantically and frustratedly kick in all directions. They will soon die if they are not found and rescued.

Some sheep are always at hand and others are notorious for becoming cast. Thomson describes the personality differences he has observed in sheep:

> Some sheep always keep near the shepherd, and are his special favourites. Each of them has a name, to which it answers joyfully; and the kind shepherd is ever distributing to such choice portions which he gathers for that purpose. These are the contented and happy ones. They are in no danger of getting lost or into mischief, nor do wild beasts or thieves come near them. The great body, however, are mere worldlings, intent upon their own pleasures or selfish interests. They run from bush to bush, searching for variety or delicacies, and only now and then lift their heads to see where the shepherd is, or rather, where the general flock is, least they get so far away as to occasion remark in their little community, or rebuke from their keeper. Others, again, are restless and discontented, jumping into everybody's field, climbing into bushes, and even into leaning trees, whence they often fall and break their limbs. These cost the good shepherd incessant trouble. Then there are others incurably restless, who stray away and are utterly lost. (*The Land and the Book*, p. 203)

Jesus' parable about the lost sheep was drawn from real life. If the shepherd finds a sheep or two missing at evening when they pass under his rod to enter the fold, he must go out immediately to seek them. Even a few hours can mean death and, dead or alive, cast sheep are easy prey to vultures, cougars, wolves and other enemies.

The shepherd searches until he finds the sheep. If the sheep is cast, he approaches with gentleness, straddling it with his feet as he slowly lifts the sheep to its feet. Using soothing but scolding words, he gently places the sheep on its numb legs and carefully massages them to restore circulation. The distraught sheep may fall again because its legs are shaky. But the shepherd patiently sets it up each time it falls until eventually it is able to stand on its own feet.

All of us who wander away become disquieted, depressed, and in need of restoration. This is why the Apostle Paul advised us to keep track of one another: "Brethren, if a man be overtaken in a fault, ye which are spiritual, restore such an one in the spirit of meekness; considering thyself, lest thou also be tempted" (Gal. 6:1).

Wandering sheep are a universal problem. We have them in our church. After their conversion, they have a fervency for God. They attend every Wednesday night service, twice on Sunday, and fit in as many extra meetings as they can. They volunteer for everything. They will tend the parking lot, shovel snow, change diapers, wash dishes—anything, just to be with the other sheep. But, after a while, they begin to cool and it's not long before we find them on their backs dying.

Restoration Ministry

They need help, and I cannot get to them all. This is where the restoration ministry of elders, deacons, and teachers is so necessary. They know when someone close to them is not walking with the Lord as he once did and is on his back about to give up.

In the average church if one of the sheep becomes discontented and wanders off, the pastor goes to that one and attempts to persuade him to return. But this is not always best. I often find it more effective to call a friend of the wanderer and ask him to talk the matter over and get back to me. Sometimes, if the senior pastor comes to visit someone who may feel a bit guilty about their wandering, it can seem overwhelming or threatening. But if another one of the flock gently talks to him about his fault while sharing his own testimony of restoration, much is accomplished.

I feel that many local churches are never able to grow because the pastor-shepherd is unable to share restoration ministry with the rest of the flock. Our people who constitute our local churches have tasted of the wonderful grace of God and are beautiful people who desire to be used of the Lord. They have personal ways and means those of us in the leadership may not have. God wants to use these natural bridges of friendship to convey His healing and restoration to the cast sheep of the community.

But there is a preventative to wandering that accomplishes even more. If something goes wrong between me and another brother, I should go to him alone and attempt to resolve the matter (Matt. 18:15-17). If we cannot understand each other and be reconciled, then we should call in one other person with us to help. Elders should be available for such a need. Only when the person refuses to be reconciled should the matter be brought to the attention of the pastor. People should not run to their pastor about every personal grievance. Growing up includes learning how to handle personal differences in a peaceable and poised way.

Some time back I was told that one of the young men of the church was no longer attending services. I asked why and was told that he felt that no one really cared whether he was around or not. As I prayed about the matter, it seemed to me that if I went it would be just another case of a minister going after one of the flock because that was his job. The young man was going to think, "Here comes the minister. He'll tell me that God cares and he cares and everybody cares and—so what!" Instead, I asked four of the young people to see him—a couple of fellows and a couple of girls. They went. In about three days the young man was restored. He felt someone did care in a personal way.

Joy is in the Mainstream

When the Psalmist declared that there is a river to make glad the city of God, he was not only talking about the work of the Holy Spirit, but about involvement in the mainstream of things. The Holy Spirit makes us outgoing people. He stimulates everything about us until we can't help giving ourselves away. Not only does He give us new avenues of contribution to make through imparting spiritual abilities, but He touches our personalities and our natural abilities until these too find a place in the kingdom. In a simple and natural way we begin to find our own little place in the local church. We discover that we are "members in particular" and that we have a contribution to make that no one else can make. As time goes on we become comfortable in that place, and gradually our influence begins to broaden. Our circle of friends grows larger.

Keeping involved is the best insurance against becoming a cast sheep. It keeps us in touch with the other sheep. We will not be off by ourselves with our hurts and depression.

Most of our people work a full hard day. They need to do more than just attend services or meetings. So, in addition to our elaborate program of Christian education, we have a highly developed sports program, classes in arts and crafts, outings, and other groups for special purposes. Participation in these groups is an important safeguard against becoming cast down and lonely.

Some people are naturally outgoing and effervescent. But others seem to drive people away. The more they long for companionship, the more their own anxieties repel the people they most want to attract. They need help to learn how to relate.

Lonely people often find friendship by serving along with others. In a large work such as ours, funerals, weddings, and special occasions abound. We always need people to prepare rooms, cook meals, set tables, and clean up. When lonely people come and give, they often find others giving them love and appreciation.

Unmarried people who do not have families or partners find it more difficult socially. Recently some of our people became aware of the lack these people experience and they decided to do something about it. They organized a group they called "The Family of God" for the many widowed, divorced, and single people of the congregation. Not only do they plan parties at holiday time and other pleasant outings, but they help each other with housecleaning, babysitting, and other practical concerns. Many people who were cast sheep for years are finding themselves useful and sought out.

Many problems that make us cast down simply fly out the window when we get busy serving others. As pastor-shepherds, one of the best things we can do in the area of releasing the sheep from being cast down is to show them opportunities for being involved. Discovery by experience that others can like them and want them around will do for them what hours of counseling could never accomplish.

CHAPTER 13

Healing Harassed Sheep

Sheep and Christians have enemies. Wolves, snakes, men and lions all threaten sheep in real and serious ways. And they are legitimately afraid of these marauders. Wolves strike such terror in sheep that a herd often refuses to even pass over the buried remains of a wolf. And, indeed, without the shepherd, they are helpless against predators.

God's people have enemies too and we are equally fearful by nature. It would be convenient if God would simply eliminate all our enemies. But this is not what He does. He does not even remove from our path occasions to fear. God's way is to make us overcomers, and this means that He works in us instead of removing our circumstances. He places in us the spiritual backbone to face up to our conflicts and fears. He enables us to stand up to life.

Pastor-shepherds have the task of educating God's people. God does not think as we do; He never has. We must learn how to flow with life as He has made it. We must adjust to the universe since God is not going to adjust it to suit us. But so many of God's people have the idea that life will now be rosy and without conflict. They often become offended because God still allows them to have problems and difficulties. They do not realize that part of God's salvation is retraining in how to live life. God insists that we learn how to slide with the grain so that we stop gathering splinters. God brings us change through every day situations.

As pastor-shepherds we must teach people how to handle the fact that we have enemies. When these enemies are people, we must learn how to transform them from enemies into friends. We must learn in practical ways how to love our enemies and to bless those who have hurt us the most. In counseling God's sheep, I cannot tell them that they have no cause for fear, that God will remove all enemies and obstacles, but I can tell them that the grace of God which has been placed within them in the person of the Holy Spirit is sufficient to enable them to stand up to any situation. God can make something out of them by using the people and situations they fear.

So many times when sheep have a problem, they think they are alone. They are sure that no one else ever faced such a crisis. It is usually my first task to reassure people that their problems are really quite commonplace. It is normal for Christians to encounter enemies and situations which require God's strength within. I often point them to David. Listen to his complaint in Psalm 22, for example:

> My God, my God, why hast thou forsaken me? why art thou so far from helping me, and from the words of my roaring? O my God, I cry in the daytime, but thou hearest not; and in the night season, and am not silent . . . I am poured out like water, and all my bones are out of joint: my heart is like wax; it is melted in the midst of my bowels. My strength is dried up like a potsherd; and my tongue cleaveth to my jaws; and thou hast brought me into the dust of death. For dogs have compassed me: the assembly of the wicked have inclosed me: they pierced my hands and my feet. (1-2;14-16)

What is David saying? "I've cried night and day to God and nothing seems to change. I've got more enemies than a dog has fleas! They seem to be all around me; I can't get away from them. They laugh at my faith. They mock my confidence in God. They say, 'Where is this God who will do so much for you?'

David had the tendency to be cast down. We would say he was suffering from a mild depression or had a touch of melancholy and needed some coffee before breakfast. Just as the shepherd anoints his sheep with oil to deal with snakebite and other injuries inflicted by enemies, so the Lord ministers to the wounds inflicted by the enemies of God's people. He does this both through the direct comfort of the Holy Spirit and through the ministry of His servants. Pastor-shepherds often have the job of healing the results of an encounter with enemies, and teaching the sheep how to handle the situation better the next time.

Sometimes the sheep injure each other. Competition and jealousy cause the sheep to butt and wound each other. In the church most wounds are inflicted by the tongue. Often we must help people overcome the results of conflict and teach them how to rightly relate to each other. We must anoint their heads with oil and ask the Holy Spirit to enter the hurt places and heal.

Anointing The Head Deals With Pests

When we listen to a person complaining as David did, we recognize that something has happened to the head—to the thinking. David was cast down and forlorn, full of self-pity and despair. He needed some real healing.

Oil is the biblical symbol for the Holy Spirit. The Holy Spirit is God working in us and upon us at the deepest possible level. His work is primarily within the mind and heart. The Holy Spirit alters our thinking and emotions.

Jesus spoke of some of the changes the Holy Spirit would bring in our thinking: the deep persuasion of sin, of righteousness, and of judgment (John 16:7-11). He convinces us of our acceptance with

God as His own dear children. Paul described this aspect of the Spirit's work as a release from fear into deep security in God's family. He used these words:

> For as many as are led by the Spirit of God, they are the sons of God. For ye have not received the spirit of bondage again to fear; but ye have received the Spirit of adoption, whereby we cry, Abba, Father. The Spirit itself beareth witness with our spirit, that we are the children of God: And if children, then heirs; heirs of God, and joint-heirs with Christ. . . . (Rom. 8:14-17)

The Holy Spirit applies the blood of Jesus to the heart and mind, purifying our conscience from guilt and dead works. The Holy Spirit writes the word of God in the fleshly tables of the heart and mind, bringing us into possession of truth. He anoints our head with oil to heal and adjust our thinking.

David is speaking in Psalm 23 as a sheep. He is describing the Great Shepherd's ministry toward him. At an important juncture in his life, the Lord anointed David's head. David was healed. These six verses are his shout of victory, "He anointed my head with oil and I am free from these thoughts that harassed me for so long."

Sheep have constant problems with pests. The summer brings insects. Sheep attract certain kinds of flies and bugs in much the same way that people draw mosquitoes.

One kind of fly will make its way into the sheeps' nostrils and lay eggs. When these hatch, the insects crawl up the nasal passages into the head. There they buzz until the sheep are absolutely confounded. They become so distracted and tormented that they will butt their heads against trees, walls, bushes—anything to stop the internal torment. They even butt each other in a desperate attempt to rid themselves of this inner distraction.

Sheep must feel the way David sounded when he wrote Psalm 22. David wrote like a man who had flies up his nose, buzzing and distracting him. He needed his head anointed.

The Oriental shepherd mixes olive oil with a pitch or turpentine base and some sulphur to make this anointing oil. It smells terrible. He places this awful smelling concoction around the sheep's nose, mouth, and eyes to destroy these pests and ward off others. You can almost hear the sheep saying with gratitude, "He anoints my head with oil, my cup runneth over. . . ."

I have discovered that pests can be either thoughts or people. Both can pester you until you need an anointing. This is an important area of ministry for the pastor-shepherd. Periodically we observe people being pestered or harassed—deeply troubled. They don't sing any more. They are uneasy. You can see it on their faces.

Common Harassing Thoughts

Let me run down a list of pests that can trouble the sheep of God. These are the complaints I hear most often in our counseling sessions.

Pest number one is condemnation. This pest nags the Christian with thoughts such as, "You don't really belong; you haven't done enough to deserve God's grace. You're not much of a Christian. . . ." Every sheep knows secret things about himself. It is so easy to condemn ourselves.

Most people condemn themselves for not doing something. They have the sneaky uneasy feeling that something ought to be done, but they do not know what it is. This false condemnation must be swept away. This pest must be destroyed.

God is not a God of condemnation. If God had any condemnation in His nature, we would all be sunk. God has every reason in the world to condemn us: we fail, we don't do what we should do, we do what we should not do. But He is merciful and gracious. The Bible tells us:

> For God sent not his Son into the world to condemn the world; but that the world through him might be saved. (John 3:17)
>
> There is therefore now no condemnation to them which

> are in Christ Jesus, who walk not after the flesh, but after the Spirit. (Rom. 8:1)

Don't allow condemnation to crawl up your nose. God's mercies are new and fresh every morning. Draw on these.

Overcome Condemnation By Blessing Others

As pastor-shepherds working along with Jesus the Great Shepherd, we learn how to apply the precise anointing that will dispel the pests. It takes more than a blanket prayer and a pat on the head. Pastor-shepherds learn by living life. I can help people deal with the flies of condemnation because I received ministry from the Holy Spirit for my own need.

A number of years ago I experienced a real release from the nagging pest of inner condemnation. It came about through the direct ministry of the Great Shepherd as He anointed my head with fresh truth and insight. I knew something was ailing me, but I didn't know what the pesky thing was. One evening I was waiting on God and reading the Bible, and it seemed like these words jumped off the page: "Bless your enemies, bless them who despitefully use you and hate you and persecute you for righteousness sake." Bless everybody! I didn't know whether I could do this or not.

In that quiet moment, I found the Holy Spirit teaching me. He said, "Bless everybody you love just like you blessed them when you were a kid." He brought to my mind our childhood training to pray, "Now I Lay Me Down to Sleep" and bless everyone before going to bed. The Lord was teaching me that I should begin by blessing everyone I found it easy to bless. Then when I was finished blessing those I felt deserved to be blessed, I was to go on and bless those I didn't particularly want to have blessed.

I was to bring to mind all the people who made me feel uneasy. I did my best to recall each one and bless him. Ooh, it's hard to bless your enemies! I would prefer to see God zap them and get them out of my way.

Certain people I didn't care to think about came to mind. I remember how hard it was to pray for one person in particular. Finally I got it out of my mouth—I choked on it. I said, "Lord, if I bless him, I'm a hypocrite. I don't want to bless him and I have no intention of blessing him." I knew my feelings were lodged deeply inside. This resentment I had against that person was clogging my life with condemnation. I was condemning him and the condemnation was returning to me. Finally, I said it, "Lord, bless him, increase him, favor him in every way."

I remember how I felt when I went to bed that night. The weight of the world had rolled off my shoulders. The next day was beautiful. I had learned that if I bless with the same measure I mete out to others, it will be measured back to me again.

Other Common Pests

Pest number two is a common fly named discontent. Scores of people fail to enjoy what they have because of what they don't have. They cannot relax in the arms of God's goodness today, because they are itching and restless about tomorrow.

Discontent comes easily to sheep who are not involved in creative pursuits within the flock. These are the sheep who feel the grass is always greener on the other side of the fence. As a result they wander from one local church to another. They are discontent and irritable and they are convinced that it is the fault of eveyone else.

The Apostle Paul said a mouthful when he declared:

> . . . for I have learned, in whatsoever state I am, therewith to be content. (Phil. 4:11)

It is necessary at times to seek the help of your pastor-shepherd in eliminating the pest of discontent. This crawling insect will make you dissatisfied with your Bible class, the choir, your prayer group, your pastor-shepherd, your friends. If you will examine yourself closely, you will discover that the pest of discontent has been troubling you and it is not these other people at all.

The day you discover that you have entered a season of discontent, run quickly for help. Discontent will take away your joy and vitality.

As sheep of God's pasture, learn to enjoy God and His goodness. Sing through the day. Before you go to bed at night, sort out your problems. Get rid of everything negative. Place it in God's hands and go to sleep. Go to sleep with a clear conscience. Then arise in the morning glorying that the day has arrived. Begin to sing as you swing your feet out of bed. "This is the day that the Lord has made, I will rejoice and be glad in it." Leave yesterday and don't anticipate tomorrow's troubles.

A third pest is the nagging suspicion that we are not "spiritual enough." People come to me and say with great concern, "Brother Jim, I'm really worried; I can't be spiritual. I'm not a spiritual person."

I ask them, "What would it feel like to be spiritual?"

They hem and haw and look at the floor. Then they begin to laugh with relief. They realize that there isn't any such feeling. Spirituality is like humility. The moment you know you are humble, you are not. Spirituality is a hidden indefinable quality. It is basically the sense of well-being—all is clear between you and the Lord. It is well with my soul.

Most people feel spiritually inadequate because of comparison. Why don't they have the faith of an Oral Roberts? The reason is: they are not Oral Roberts! Each of us can be himself and enjoy each level of growth and development. There is no telling what you will be if you cease putting limitations on your life. Why would you want to be like anyone else? That would only make you a second-rate person. Spirituality and spiritual development are not the same. A new born babe can be as spiritual as an eighty-year-old saint. The babe cannot do what the older person can, but his state of spirituality can be the same if he is walking before the Lord in harmony and fellowship.

The Problem of Contagion

Undershepherds should intervene quickly when they observe sheep being troubled. Pests are contagious. They spread quickly through the entire flock if immediate action is not taken.

One extremely contagious pest in the local church is bitterness. If people do not handle discontent and anger immediately, it develops into a deep resentment that becomes corrosive not only to themselves but to all around them. Bitter people live in a world of distortion and their talk reflects this. Every word carries a degree of contamination. The writer to the Hebrews spoke of this problem:

> Follow peace with all men, and holiness, without which no man shall see the Lord: looking diligently lest any man fail of the grace of God; lest any root of bitterness springing up trouble you, and thereby many be defiled. (12:14-15)

When people begin to show signs of discouragement and frustration, we see it in their faces. While visiting in New Zealand, I noticed a flock of sheep with facial eczema. This rash came as a result of a liver condition. The shepherds marked these sheep with a swipe of yellow paint on the top of their heads and one side. In this way, they could keep an eye on their progress. They carried the mark of sickness.

If this sickness progressed, the sheep, of necessity, had to be isolated and placed in another paddock. This was done so he or she could receive special care and medication, and also to eliminate the possibility of contagion to the entire flock.

In the same way, sheep of the local church congregation must be observed and, if sickness is seen, the scrutiny must be intensified. Often the sheep will find healing through time and feeding. But, if the condition steadily worsens, they must be separated from the flock to receive special counseling. It has been my observation that a pastor-shepherd who is weak in counseling finds his flock seriously contaminated from time to time.

CHAPTER 14

Sheep Need a Leader

Sheep need a leader—a shepherd. People were made to be governed. The instinct to follow a leader is as ingrained in sheep as the instinct to lead is ingrained in a leader. This is the natural order of things. It is probably this fact that prompted God to equate His people with sheep. Deep contentment is only possible for people and for animals when their basic needs are satisfied. If the need to be governed is not met, the result is confusion and frustration.

If men do not have leadership, they will create it. We see this happen all the time. Watch the boys as they go out to play baseball. You cannot play ball without organization, rules, and leadership. Somebody is going to choose sides and set up teams. They will say, "Hey, you, you be captain!" They will holler to the other fellow, "Joe, you be captain!" Have you noticed that the same guys are captains all the time? People select their own leaders. This is as normal as breathing.

This setting up of government is natural among the animals too. In the chicken yard, roosters establish leadership by subduing their opponents. This is called the "pecking order." The rooster who can out-peck all the others is the undisputed head of the coop—that is, until another arises who can out-peck him. Animals with antlers, such as deer and moose, establish a "horning order." And as you might expect, sheep and goats have a "butting order." Leadership emerges from competition. Those who excel become the leaders.

Since the need for a leader is so great, people will even follow those who care little for their interests. Like sheep, people are essentially "followers." If someone is leading, it is natural to follow. People have a deep fear of being left without direction. They do not want to be left on their own. Bad government is preferable to no government. Bad leadership is better than anarchy.

From early times, men have looked upon both their human leaders and the gods as "shepherds."

People Will Make Their Own Leaders

If the shepherds God intends to use to lead His people fail to rise to His call, the people will take matters into their own hands. If God's chosen leaders do not emerge, the herd will select one of their own to lead them. People need government so badly that they will create it on their own.

It is God's responsibility to call and prepare gifted leaders for the local church. Often we forget this. We are prone to rush. We must get the show on the road. The place and scope of leadership is the source of much confusion in the church-world of today. Regrettably, the charismatic quality so needed in leadership is not insisted upon by church officials. Putting a man behind a pulpit does not automatically change him into God's man for the situation.

Today's church-world is presently facing a challenge regarding this whole area of leadership. We are in transition. The denominational churches have seen strong men and women emerge from the ranks with significant ministries. These charismatic leaders have led tens of thousands into fresh and new experiences with God. Many have been miraculously healed through their ministries. Others have been filled with the Spirit and stirred deeply. Businessmen testify of the grace of God and what the Holy Spirit has done for them. But these leaders are not pastor-shepherds. God never intended them to be. Now the sheep are searching for settled and established local church leadership to guide them day by day through the pastures of God's word. They are looking for examples to show them how to apply biblical principles to every day life.

It is at this point that the Holy Spirit must intervene. He must call and prepare pastor-shepherds. If the Holy Spirit does not call men and women into the ministry and make them gifts to the church, we are left with human church government. We have had this for centuries and we can't live with it any more. It is like dust in our mouths; we can't swallow it.

In every generation God has His called leaders, but usually they are unrecognized by the masses. Consequently, the people choose their leaders by application of their own yardstick. We keep falling into the same deception as did our fathers: namely, that we know more than God when people are involved.

Jesus' disciples evidently spent considerable time thinking about the kingdom of God during the three and a half years they walked with the Master. But the problem was that their thoughts of the kingdom did not coincide with what Jesus knew it to be. The squabbles they had among themselves had to do with which of them was the greatest. On these occasions Jesus would patiently but firmly explain the true meaning of leadership. For example, in Luke 22:24-27 we read:

> And there was also a strife among them, which of them should be accounted the greatest. And he said unto them, The kings of the Gentiles exercise lordship over them; and they that exercise authority upon them are called benefactors. But ye shall not be so: but he that is greatest among you, let him be as the younger; and he that is chief, as he that doth serve.

Jesus was speaking of government and leadership familiar to the disciples. He contrasted Gentile government to the kingdom of God. They simply were worlds apart.

Jesus' term "benefactor" was not original. He was using the political vernacular of His day. The Greeks had made this concept of benefactor popular. Their famous philosopher Plato had written what is probably the greatest discourse on human government. It is called *The Republic*. Not only had Plato's ideas greatly influenced the people of his day, but his writings are still required reading for most high school and college students. Most other important writing about government has been influenced by Plato's *Republic*.

Plato was not inventing theory as much as he was observing how men did things. He observed much the same thing Jesus said to His disciples: People will make their own leaders because they demand leadership. They will call these leaders benefactors because they believe in the benefits provided through government.

Plato went into considerable detail describing the way men make their own leaders. If they do not have leadership, they will select one of their own and nurse him to greatness. While they are nursing him to greatness, they consider him an asset and call him their benefactor.

But after a while this benefactor does something that changes him from a benefactor into a tyrant. This change begins in the leader's own thinking. The change in his mental processes is this: "I have power over these people because they look to me; I could make them serve me instead of my serving them." And the leader starts serving himself.

The moment a leader ceases serving the people and becomes self-serving, the seeds of tyranny are planted. In time, tyranny produces revolution. The populace soon realizes that this man must be pulled down from his pinnacle of power. The same society who nursed this leader to greatness will also pull him down.

This process will be repeated in a church if the leader was placed there through human means rather than by God's sovereign setting of a "gift" in place. If the people "made" the pastor-shepherd, they can also recall him. An elected pastor-shepherd can easily be replaced in the next election. At first they say, "This is our man, our pastor!" But usually the honeymoon is a short-lived one.

Sheep Without Shepherds

So basic is our need for leadership that on several occasions the Bible records prayers and statements that people without leaders are as "sheep without shepherds." If something happens to leadership, the people cannot function together as a united group. Everything falls apart. Like Zechariah the prophet said:

> . . . smite the shepherd, and the sheep shall be scattered. (13:7)

Instinctively we know this and fear being left to ourselves and our waywardness.

One of the greatest prayers in Scripture is that of Moses in Numbers 27:16-17:

> Let the LORD, the God of the spirits of all flesh, set a man over the congregation, which may go out before them, and which may go in before them, and which may lead them out, and which may bring them in; that the congregation of the LORD be not as sheep which have no shepherd.

Moses' prayer embraces four basic purposes for pastoral leadership. They are listed in these verb phrases:

(1) may go out before them;
(2) may go in before them;
(3) may lead them out;
(4) may bring them in.

Moses—an experienced shepherd himself—knew that this balance in leadership was essential to the survival of the flock. It was not enough for the leader to be skilled in one area, he must function in all governmental aspects.

These action phrases have specific meaning. They were not words thrown together without rhyme or reason. They were military expressions and terms describing the right to initiate that rested within a king or general by virtue of his position. The combined ideas of going in and coming out convey the assurance that the leader of God's people will see them through from start to finish. He will not desert them in midstream.

God's Leaders First Set An Example

Moses first spoke of leaders going out before the people. They went out first and made the trail for others to follow. They surveyed the situation and established the way to go. This is done primarily through personal experience which becomes the pattern for others to follow. All through the Scriptures we find that God required of His leaders the ability to live an exemplary life. Paul exhorted Timothy in charging him with leadership responsibility.

> . . . be thou an example of the believers, in word, in conversation, in charity, in spirit, in faith, in purity. (1 Tim. 4:12)

Peter set himself up as an example and then spoke with authority to other leaders not to dominate as "lords" but to make others want to follow their example:

> Neither as being lords over God's heritage, but being ensamples to the flock. (1 Pet. 5:3)

Leaders can only "lead" if others will follow them. In order to attract followers, leaders must somehow inspire people to emulate their own example. There is no doubt about it; every true leader inspires other people to be like him. This is precisely why we want to be like Jesus—He is our Leader, our Shepherd.

I find that wanting to be like other people is normal and in tune with reality. If I am listening to someone sing who has great talent, I want to sing in the same way. I remember when I was a boy and would go to see a band play. I watched the cornet players and the people who did so well on the clarinets. I wanted to go home, pick up one of these instruments, and play just like they had. I think all of us as children daydreamed about doing this because it looked so easy.

The same is true about pastor-shepherds who have confidence and poise and who are able to minister the word of God almost effortlessly. We want to do the same thing. A good pastor-shepherd produces leaders who emulate him and want to be just like he is. Someone has said that the greatest form of flattery is imitation. In a very real sense, it is.

God's Leaders Motivate Others To Enter Into Life

The next thing Moses said a leader must do was to "go in before" the people. He would be the first to encounter any new situation or to confront any difficulties. One good example of such a leader is Joshua. He and Caleb were the only ones allowed to go into the promised land after the unbelief and murmuring stirred God's wrath against His people at Kadesh-Barnea. Their attitude of enthusiastic faith and courage was such that they could lead others into the land. Their own confidence in God was exemplary and motivated others to follow. Joshua could take the people in when Moses could not. Moses had allowed the people to pressure his reactions. Joshua instead determined the attitude of the entire camp: he was full of cheer and confidence because his faith was anchored deep in God. His enthusiasm became contagious.

God's leaders motivate the people to enter into life in much the same way that Joshua took the people in to possess their inheritance in Canaan. The leader's emotional tone sets the attitude of the whole flock. If the leader of the church is happy, outgoing, and inventive, again the people want to be as he is. I feel that some leaders repel folks from the church. They always have the look of being distressed and defeated. They never give the impression that their job is one that they relish and thoroughly enjoy.

When I come into our services on Sunday morning, Sunday evening, or Wednesday night, I go to the pulpit as a man who enjoys his job. As I have the people stand, I usually say, "This is the day that the Lord has made, we will rejoice and be glad in it." If I am rejoicing, in time they are going to rejoicing. If I look like the weight of the world is on my shoulders, they will want to carry a part of that load with me and therefore share in my depression. If I am a man of faith, I motivate others to faith. If I am a man who loves to sing, the congregation will be a singing church.

I have especially noticed that when the pastor-shepherd does not participate in the singing or really open his life to praise, that church is not a singing and praising church. The sheep feel that in some way if this were the thing to do, their own pastor-shepherd would enter into it with gusto. Since he has reservations, they are reluctant to go ahead. They are not motivated to do what he demonstrates hesitancy about doing.

I have made it a habit in all of our services—especially when we have an evangelist with us—to sit with the guest speaker on the platform so that the people can see my face. I believe that they need to see my face. If I am receiving what the man or woman has to say, they are able to receive it eagerly as well. But if they see my reluctance or hesitation, and if they read a question in my face then they are not apt to eat the food that he is presenting. You might say, "This does not seem fair."

But I say in return, "This is part of the pastoral care of the sheep." The sheep will know whether or not to eat the food set before them by whether their pastor-shepherd is eager and responsive. He motivates even their appetite.

God's Leaders Direct And Coordinate Others

The third task of the leader, according to Moses, is to set the pace, be first in rank, or as the Scripture puts it, "lead them out." The leader always has a staff of some kind—a stick which symbolizes the pointing of the way for others to follow and the authority to discipline. We see this in the shepherd's staff. We see it with military and police billy clubs. Even our generals carry sticks. In the field of music we find the same thing: both the conductor and the drum major use a baton.

The leader sets the tempo and the direction. He stands before the group to get them started, to keep them in unison, and to inspire confidence. He keeps time. I call this "the right of initiative."

I believe that in any group of people, whether in a sheepfold or in a civic organization, there must be somebody who sparks the meeting into motion. This may be the man who pounds the gavel. It may be the man who shoots the gun to set off the race. It may be the pastor-shepherd who walks to the pulpit and says, "Shall we all stand for prayer and begin our service." People need leadership. They need somebody to initiate the program. I feel that the pastor-shepherd is the normal initiator; he leads the way and the sheep follow.

In our song services, we need somebody to say, "Turn to hymn number 38 and we will sing all four verses." Someone is getting us started on the downbeat. This is the way it is all through life. Someone initiates, and I believe it is the pastor-shepherd and not the church board. Naturally the church board will have something to say about the initiative when it involves large decisions, but in the total work of the church there must be leadership and the right of initiative must fall into the hands of that God-appointed leader.

God's Leaders Develop Others And Set Them In Place

Moses' final phrase describing the activity of God's leaders was that they "may bring them in"—that is, cause God's people to find fruition and fulfillment. Joshua divided the land of Canaan into portions and made sure that every tribe, family, and individual received an inheritance. We all have an inheritance in Christ—a spiritual possession to possess. God's leaders under the direction of the Holy Spirit bring us to the realization of that place in God.

It is normal for the pastor-shepherd to watch his flock and to know where particular talents lie. Some men can do one job well, whereas they cannot do another. Some men are naturally more personable than others. When there is a need for leadership, it seems normal that the pastor-shepherd seek out from among the flock and select good leaders with fine godly attributes, talents, and spiritual gifts.

You will notice in the Epistles to Timothy and to Titus that the Apostle Paul gives the right of initiative to both of these evangelists. He said that wherever they went and into whatsoever city they entered, they had the responsibility of selecting elders—but they must be careful who they chose. Titus was warned when he went to Crete that the Cretans had certain national traits that were not desirable. For this reason, he must carefully pick out from among these men only those who met certain qualifications. He was not to put a man into the place of leadership who would bring reproach on the church of Jesus Christ.

You will notice in the evangelistic Epistles of Timothy and Titus that the right of initiative and the right of selection did not fall into the hands of the congregation. These evangelists were serving as pastor-shepherds at that particular time. As these local churches developed, no doubt the pastor-shepherd gift would emerge from among them. Then the new leader would have the responsibility of seeing that proper leadership came into the various areas of the church.

Leaders must not be set into the church as the result of a popularity contest. Leaders in the church must be selected through fasting and prayer—that is, we must have the mind of God about certain men and women who will take their places of needed leadership.

CHAPTER 15

Government—What Is It?

Government is social control which makes it possible for people to live together in peace. In order to have any kind of government at least three things are involved:

(1) a territory

(2) a people

(3) leadership

The territory of God's government is the local church. To be sure, He is Lord over the entire church, but when it comes to practical expression of God's government, we find it within each local sheepfold.

We find no biblical warrant for the merging of local churches under any hierarchy. The bond between local churches is one of fellowship and unity of the Spirit—not of government. The local church at Jerusalem did not dictate policy to the church in Rome, and Rome did not establish policy in Corinth.

God has limited His direct, personal rule to those who have submitted to His kingdom. Only those who have entered through Christ, the Door, are members of the sheepfold and eligible for the Shepherd's care and rule. God makes no attempt during this dispensation to rule the heathen except through providence and through prayers of His people. His personal rule is presently "within" individual hearts. It is experienced by those who are now in His kingdom, the active sphere of His reign.

God has appointed leaders within His church to act as undershepherds in each local church. He had endowed His leaders with a "charisma" not only for gathering the sheep, but for governing them.

Basic to government is community. By community we mean that commonality which binds us together despite our individual diversity. God's Spirit joins us to one another until we experience unity at the deepest possible level. By living for common goals, developing a common language, and following common leaders, we become "one." We experience a deep sense of oneness and knowledge that collectively "we" are somebody, which we call *esprit de corps*.

Anthropologists tell us that basically there are five possible types of human government.

(1) Oligarchy—the government by an elite few.
(2) Monarchy—government by one man or woman.
(3) Gerontocracy—government by the old men.
(4) Democracy—government by a large portion of the people, usually through some form of representation.
(5) Theocracy (or hierarchy)—government by God through appointed authorities.

All through Scripture, we find theocracy designated as the personal rule of God over His redeemed community. This is as true in the church of Jesus Christ as it was in the nation of Israel.

All Authority Is Of God

God's people live in His kingdom and are subject to Christ as King. They are to obey His delegated authorities in the church. But they also live in the natural world with its own political systems. God's people do not live together in a physical and political community of their own and enjoy immunity from the laws of the land. God's people are scattered throughout the world under every sort of human government.

God's people are a people with a dual citizenship. They are duty bound by God's word to submit to whatever form of natural government their society exercises. As subjects of His kingdom they are also required to obey Jesus Christ as Lord, and this includes obeying those He sets over them in the church. These are simultaneous; they must render both to Caesar and to Christ.

God has prevented conflict in the area of authority and obedience by requiring His subjects to obey all authorities as unto Him—even when they are bad rulers appointed by men. The Apostle Paul in writing to the Romans removed any doubt about this. He said:

> Obey the government, for God is the one who has put it there. There is no government anywhere that God has not placed in power. So those who refuse to obey the laws of the land are refusing to obey God, and punishment will follow. For the policeman does not frighten people who are doing right; but those doing evil will always fear him. So if you don't want to be afraid, keep the laws and you will get along well. The policeman is sent by God to help you. But if you are doing something wrong, of course you should be afraid, for he will have you punished. He is sent by God for that very purpose. Obey the laws, then, for two reasons: first, to keep from being punished, and second, just because you should. Pay your taxes too, for these same two reasons. For government workers need to be paid so that they can keep on doing God's work, serving you. (13:1-7 TLB)

Nothing could be plainer: God's subjects must submit to human government as part of their obedience to God.

The church, as we have said, is a society of its own imposed upon the natural social order. It is a community within a community, a nation within a nation. The government of the church is quite different from the government of the social order. Problems arise when God's people forget this and try to incorporate ideas and attitudes derived from human forms of government. When they try to run the church like the P.T.A., everybody is in trouble. God designed His church to be the territory of His personal rule—His kingdom—a theocracy! This may exist in a social order under monarchy, oligarchy, gerontocracy, or democracy. God's people must learn when to render unto God and when to Caesar.

All the forms of human government have advantages as well as disadvantages. If there were no good points to these types of political structures, people would not have devised these means for governing themselves. But this does not authorize us to borrow and incorporate democratic ideals, or the simplicity of single-man monarchy, or any other human structures. God has already made known His rule in terms of theocracy. He is Lord!

Keeping God First Is Not Easy

When we live in a society it is easy to be poured into its mold of ideas and values. It is a part of our herding instinct to want to do things just like our neighbors do them. They buy a new car and we must have one. They remodel their home and we become dissatisfied with our own. We become copycats easily. This same pressure comes upon us regarding government. If all the other nations have a king to lead them out to battle, then we must have one too. This was the whole problem about Israel's setting up of Saul. They were rejecting God's order—theocracy—in order to copy the human form of government their neighbors had—monarchy. When Samuel complained to God, he was told:

> Hearken unto the voice of the people in all that they say unto thee: for they have not rejected thee, but they have rejected me, that I should not reign over them. (1 Sam. 8:7)

The church has not done much better than Israel did in this matter. It has passed through repeated cycles of renewal, prosperity and decay, and, in every instance, I believe, the reason for decay lay in the unwillingness of God's people to pay the price of truly following Christ.

Jesus Christ alone reserves the right to build the church. He alone has absolute authority in heaven and earth, and He exercises that authority through His servants. It began with the twelve apostles and has continued through the apostles, prophets, evangelists, pastors and teachers.

Christ Delegated His Own Authority

On the day of Pentecost, Peter, along with the eleven, comprised the spiritual nucleus around which the converts gathered. These apostles did not have authority because of their office, but because no one could gainsay the power of God which was working through them.

These same men took the oversight of the church and remained there until men from the congregation were matured enough to share some of the responsibility. During this time they had to do all of the work—and with over 8,120 people this was no small matter. But they faithfully waited for God to take the initiative in providing additional leadership. It was seven years before the first deacons were appointed. Even then, they were appointed only because of the evident necessity to care for the widows.

It seemed at first that the deacons were to handle practical matters of charitable distribution and the like, but, in fact, two of them, Stephen and Philip, became notable leaders in the church. Stephen had wide latitude and opportunity to minister. He went out in the streets of Jerusalem, preached Christ, and condemned the Jewish multitude for not recognizing what was happening among them spiritually. He was stoned to death—the first martyr—and, with that taste of death, a vicious persecution of the church arose throughout Jerusalem. Disciples were consequently scattered into

Judea and Samaria.

Philip was among those who escaped to Samaria and preached Christ to the people there, who marveled at the miracles that were performed through him. Many were converted and baptized. When Peter and John came down, they did not rebuke Philip for his work. They approved of what he had done and sought to complement it. They recognized Philip's converts as genuine believers and laid their hands upon them that they might receive the gift of the Holy Spirit. Obviously the apostles in authority did not inhibit the people from having the word of the Lord in their mouths and sharing it with everybody around.

The original twelve apostles (Judas replaced by Matthias) hold a unique position in the New Testament. They are not the same as the other apostles and leaders who came into the church following Pentecost. In the Book of Revelation they are called the twelve apostles of the Lamb (21:14). They are the only apostles who will ever have this special place.

Along with the twelve there were elders in the Jerusalem church (Acts 15:2), including other apostles, prophets, evangelists, pastors, and teachers.

These elders constituted all five of the ascension-ministry gifts. Among them, for example, were prophets like Barnabas, Judas and Silas. If we fail to make this distinction between the twelve apostles and the later ascension-gift apostles, we can become confused about the relationship between the apostles and the elders.

Ancient tradition says that the twelve eventually left Jerusalem (James, the brother of John, was killed, Acts 12:2) and went to various parts of the world. We know that John ended up on Patmos and Thomas is supposed to have evangelized India. Leadership of the church in Jerusalem fell to the elders who had worked with them. One of them, James, the brother of Jesus, had already achieved notable status in the church by the time of the council mentioned in Acts 15. Evidently he gained this position on the basis of his gift or charisma—his obvious authority in ministry. The other elders recognized that here was a man of God who had the gifts and talents to lead them in the work. They were pleased to submit to his authority.

When Paul was writing to the Galatians, he said that James, the Lord's brother, was one of the apostles, not one of the twelve. But I believe that he was primarily the pastor-shepherd of the church in Jerusalem. That's because, in Galatians, Paul speaks of "certain [men who] came from James." They were, in fact, from Jerusalem. The church and its leader were synonymous.

CHAPTER 16

The Gift of Government

Government in the church is never man-made; it is a gift from God, and the pastor-shepherd is one of His gifts to the local church.

Peter said:

> As every man hath received the gift, even so minister the same one to another, as good stewards of the manifold grace of God. If any man speak, let him speak as the oracles of God; if any man minister, let him do it as of the ability which God giveth: that God in all things may be glorified through Jesus Christ, to whom be praise and dominion for ever and ever. Amen. (1 Pet. 4:10-11)

God's Government Means Gifted Persons

Christ is the head of the church. But since His rule is to be carried out through men and women, the task is to insure that government remains in the hands of those gifted people God has chosen. This requires some means of recognizing those people and some way to designate them before the congregation. As long as the twelve apostles were in charge, there was little difficulty.

Once they began to pass from the scene, however, problems arose. No one could take their places. But the laying on of their hands did impart real blessing and charisma to others. By this means they set men apart to God and gave them honor in the sight of the people they were to lead. This was nothing magical. It was a spiritual transaction carried out in faith and obedience.

The appointment of leaders was never arbitrary; it was evident to all when a person was gifted by God. In the choosing of these first deacons, the apostles simply told the multitude of disciples to look within their own company and select seven men who were honest, full of the Holy Spirit, and wise. Why? This was not election on the basis of popularity, but concurrence with the choice God had already made among them. They were merely recognizing the gifts of God.

In the later chapters of Acts, we find the apostles going from city to city ordaining elders. In these new churches, they did not expect the congregation to be mature enough to recognize the leadership God was raising up from among them. The apostles could see God-given potential in men and women that was not always apparent to the young congregations of new believers. As these congregations became established under the care of local pastor-shepherds and other elders, further leadership could be drawn from the congregation by these local leaders.

All through the New Testament record we find that government was always in these charismatic rather than bureaucratic terms. Very little is said about the structure of government because the focus is on specific individuals who functioned charismatically. It was not until people lost this simple and direct relationship with Christ that they began to formulate systems of government.

They forgot that government is not a system but a gift. As a result, the early church left us a legacy of three basic forms of church government, each of which survives to this day. Each one of these forms emphasizes one aspect of the way God worked when the Holy Spirit was free to direct the church's affairs, but all of them have departed from the simplicity which we find in Christ alone.

Is there a relationship between the gospel of the kingdom which the church proclaims and the visible form it presents to the world? Jesus taught that the answer to this question was affirmative but that it would be seen in terms of practical love and loyal relationships. The further the church departed from the living presence of God, the more it answered the question by providing external structure in the form of government and architecture. Robert S. Paul makes a keen observation in his recent book *The Church In Search of Itself:*

> The classic way in which the churches have answered this question is in terms of polity—and it provides a means of classification that ranges from Roman Catholicism, with a hierarchical structure headed by the Pope as the "Bishop of bishops," to atomistic congregational independency. The three simple patterns that emerged paralleled the three basic systems of civil government known to the ancient world—episcopal (monarchical), presbyterian (oligarchic or aristocratic), and congregational (democratic). (p. 31)

The names of these types of government are derived from the word which best describes the focus of power or authority in each. The episcopal form of government centers around the bishop. The Greek word for bishop or overseer is *episkopos*. This word describes the pastor-shepherd as one who looks over and guards the flock (*skopos*: "to see or look" *epi*: over). The presbyterian form of government focuses upon a group of elders, taking the term from the greek *presbuteros*, which means "elder." According to this system, power is in the hands of several elders of equal rank, called a presbytery or session. The congregational form of government places power in the hands of the entire congregation and emphasizes the independence of each church in matters of finance and policy.

Under episcopal government, authority is conferred upon the local pastor-shepherd by those who are his superiors in an ecclesiastical hierarchy. Under presbyterian government, authority results from the concurrence of a session of elders. Under congregational government the right to rule is conferred by the choice of the people to be governed by a particular pastor-shepherd. Under none of these arrangements does the pastor-shepherd have the ultimate authority to declare the will of God for the local congregation. In every case there is a higher human authority. In this way, the pastoral charisma to rule and to administrate is limited.

Each one of these historic forms of government stresses a valid biblical point, but no one of them is the Bible pattern. Here at the Bethesda Temple we realize the importance of ultimate leadership, of a presiding elder or bishop who can make a decision for the entire congregation and speak as the voice of authority for all of the elders. But we also see the necessity for waiting until all of the elders who comprise our church council can feel that God is moving in a certain direction before proceeding in major matters. We can afford to wait for unanimity and have the sense of peace and knowledge that it is good both to the Holy Ghost and to us before acting. Nor do we overlook the voice of the people themselves. We look for their consent and response when we seek to build or to expand in new directions. We hold annual open business meetings where questions are aired. But the people do not elect their leaders; God has already appointed them. By combining the valid contributions from each stream of history, we feel that our local government has been strengthened and streamlined in efficiency.

CHAPTER 17

Vocation—the Summons from God

Anything becomes an issue because of a vacuum. The present-day contention over the pastoral ministry has arisen because there is a lack there. Any time there is a problem in the realm of leadership it is because leaders are not standing up and being counted. You always have a leadership crisis when there isn't leadership. We see this demonstrated by our national political parties. They at times have difficulty finding standard-bearers. Leaders simply do not emerge. Because of this lack, many swing swords to assert themselves as the greatest.

All through history we find that the problems which confront the nations soon confront the church as well. God intended it to be this way. Christ prayed that His people would be left "in" but not "of" the world because He wanted to use them as an instrument of social change. Bringing about this change in society at large requires that the issues be confronted and solved in the church first. Influence must grow out of example. So we find the church struggling to find God's answers to the many problems in our day about leadership, authority, and respect for government. The church is not working through these problems for itself but in order to have something workable to offer the world.

In our time we are seeing a breakdown of the family unit. As prophesied in Scripture, children have turned from their fathers (2 Tim. 3:1-5). Disrespect is rampant everywhere. This loss of respect for parents is directly related to the loss of respect for other God-given authorities. We as the family of God must rediscover how to relate to those over us in the Lord—our spiritual fathers—before we can speak with authority to society as a whole. Our verbal message will only have as much impact as our example. Respect must be restored within the church.

If everyone determines his own law, the result is anarchy, confusion, and despair. The cohesion that kept society intact dissolves. Even covenants are broken. There is no respect for family, church, or government. This is an age of "lawlessness." The Spirit of God is lifting up a standard against this flood by means of the word and by restoring the local churches as examples of order and peace. As the spirit of this age genders more and more anarchy, God's Spirit is being poured out in unprecedented measure to restore respect and obedience.

Accompanying the widespread outpouring of the Holy Spirit is a restoration of obedience to delegated authority. God is restoring the truth that He is behind all authority. Our obedience to any authority is really respect for God. The child's duty and the sheep's duty is to respect and submit to authority—even when that authority is a virtue that serves as the mortar, cementing the foundations of church and society.

Current trends in some teaching circles tend to minimize pastoral responsibility and authority. This reflects our national skepticism about leadership. National and international pressures are being reflected by parallels within the church. But because this is God's plan, we will find the Spirit arising in God's people to overcome evil with good. Answers about delegated authority and respect will first come in the community of the redeemed where true leadership comes from the Holy Spirit. God's people will serve as salt to correct and preserve society as long as they do not lose their distinctive savor by blending too much with the world's values and strategies. Paul's warning rings as clear and true today as it did when it was written to the Romans centuries ago:

> Don't let the world around you squeeze you into its mold, but let God remold your minds from within, so that you may prove in practice that the plan of God for you is good, meets all his demands and moves toward the goal of true maturity. (Rom. 12:2-3 Phillips)

The present need in our nation is leadership. We need government—good government—for without it we are disjointed and bewildered. This is also the need in the church, local and universal. This is the vacuum God is seeking to fill by redefining the role and authority of the pastor-shepherd. God is restoring the local pastor-shepherd to his rightful place as leader of the local fold—a leader to be honored, respected, and obeyed. God has given gifts to the church to fill this need for government; we are learning to recognize the pastoral charisma and to give it the respect it deserves.

We Can Overcome Disillusionment

Every time God moves afresh in history, many people become disillusioned with the institutions and doctrines of the past. When we suddenly become aware of God's original pattern, we become impatient with ourselves and fellow Christians because we find we have deviated so far from His plans. We tend to become reactionaries and swing to the opposite extreme. But we do not find this attitude in the Master Potter. When He finds a marred vessel—a creation of His hands which did not come out as He intended—He does not smash it in disgust, but He takes the time to reshape it. He is patient with us. He knows He can make something out of us that we cannot make of ourselves. He will strip away the excess, but He values the raw material of our yielded lives. He will remake the vessel as many times as necessary to fit us to His purposes.

When Juan Carlos Ortiz became disillusioned with the institutional church in Argentina, he pinpointed a real vaccum in the area of vital pastoral leadership. He became sensitive to a genuine lack in the relationship of the pastor-shepherd to his sheep. He shared this with other men in various parts of the world and in this country. They also became acutely aware of the deficiencies in present-day pastoral practices. Ortiz and his followers sounded an alarm to awaken the church to its need for restoration of personal relationships and discipline in the local church. They are calling our attention to a genuine need.

But in rushing to fill this vacuum they are falling into the same error that I have made and that many of you have made. In their disillusionment, they are making haste. They are becoming iconoclastic. They are discounting things of value in the raw material of the local church. Instead of remaking the vessels, they are seeking to do away with them. They have forgotten that God's pattern is the local church and that He still supplies His church with gifted individuals who serve as apostles, prophets, evangelists, pastors, and teachers—and that these operate in the context of the gathered community in each locality. Sheep are still fed and protected in the sheepfold where they are tended by individuals sovereignly called and equipped to care for the sheep. Decentralization into informal house groups or cells cannot take the place of the gathered community which becomes a habitation for God in the Spirit only as they come together. It is the local pastor-shepherd who has the charisma to gather the sheep in this way. Men do not become pastor-shepherds by arbitrary appointment but by the supernatural vocation of God.

Not all elders are so equipped. Not all pastor any more than all prophesy or have gifts of healing. God divides charisma severally as He wills. This means that the word "elder" is not always synonymous with "pastor-shepherd." We have many elders in our own local church, but they do not all have the pastoral gift.Some have the word of wisdom, others have the word of knowledge. Some have the healing gifts. But shepherding is not synonymous with eldership. It depends on a man's gift and vocation.

If you take a young man and set him over a group of twelve disciples, he may be lifted up with self-importance. He may become arbitrary and his pride will make him wield a sledge hammer. He is going to have disciples "or else"; people are going to submit. We must not forget that our authority is not arbitrary, neither is it ecclesiastical; our authority is spiritual. It is our ability to feed. If you divide the local church into small cells and put elders in charge of some of the sheep, but these men do not have the pastoral gift, some of the sheep simply will not be fed.

We Must Recognize Our Vocation

The poet said that "only God can make a tree." Similarly, we must recognize that only God can make a pastor-shepherd. A pastor-shepherd must have a divine vocation to gather, feed, protect, and rule sheep. Other men cannot make him a gift to the church; he must be "given" by the ascended Christ. He must have a valid pastoral vocation and give himself in preparation for fulfilling that calling. If we are to see God fill the vacuum in the area of charismatic leadership, we must let Him make the selections. We must set aside our own ideas and ideals and listen for the voice of the Chief Shepherd. He is the one who does the calling. We must take the time to be sure of His calling for us before we know how to "walk worthy" of that vocation (Eph. 4:1).

I enjoy what the Bible has to say about our calling. I like the fact that God calls us and gives us the sense of mission. I speak often about the sense of destiny because this is important to me. I am not here on my own; I am "under orders." I am acting as a delegated authority.

I remember my days in the navy. In the military we knew what it meant to be under orders. We didn't want to get to some battlefield and fight alone without instruction. I wanted to know that wherever I went I was sent under orders and that my superiors knew I was there. We needed assurances that national purposes were involved, that we were in the Pacific for valid reasons, and that others would back us. We needed answers.

When we are called by God we know it, and we know why we are assigned to specific localities and situations. We are never acting on our own.

This matter of vocation is not meant to be a mystery. It is as clear-cut and practical as any military assignment. When we are under orders this means that we know what God is asking of us. We know what His orders are. There need be no question in our mind as to whether or not we have a vocation.

Allow me to refresh your memory by spelling out what the word "vocation" means. This is one of many religious terms that has lost its original simple meaning. Vocation comes from the Latin verb *vocatio* which means: "summons, bidding, or invitation." God does the summoning or inviting, and we respond to His initiative. We do not decide with some "vocational guidance counselor" that the pastoral ministry would make a good career. Either God calls us to Himself and to this work and "gives" us to His people with the ability to gather and to feed, or we have no such vocation. This emphasis upon divine initiative is clearly stressed in Webster's dictionary definitions of the term:

(1) Vocation is a summons from God to an individual (or group) to undertake the obligations and to perform the duties of a particular task or function in life.

(2) Vocation is a divine call to a place of service to others in accordance with the divine plan. It is the carrying out of orders.

(3) Vocation is a divine call to a religious career such as the priesthood or pastoral ministry as shown by one's fitness, natural inclinations, and conviction of divine summons.

Let's keep these basic definitions in mind as we explore the biblical evidence that will show us and others whether or not we have such a God-given vocation.

The Called Pastor-Shepherd Knows His Calling

When God lays His hand upon us for any kind of ministry, we know it. We are so sure inside that no one can persuade us otherwise. To be sure, we all experience seasons of temptation to question and doubt the purpose of God for our lives, but underneath it all in our hearts there is a sureness, a knowledge that the Holy Spirit has placed there. No man can take that knowledge from us.

The story of Elijah and the call of Elisha serves as an excellent illustration of what we mean by knowledge of calling. We find this story in 1 Kings 19:19-21. In the Living Bible it reads this way:

> So Elijah went and found Elisha who was plowing a field with eleven other teams ahead of him; he was at the end of the line with the last team. Elijah went over to him and threw his coat across his shoulders and walked away again. Elisha left the oxen standing there and ran after Elijah and said to him, "First let me go and say good-bye to my father and mother, and then I'll go with you!" Elijah replied, "Go on back! Why all the excitement?" Elisha then returned to his oxen, killed them, and used wood from the plow to build a fire to roast their flesh. He passed around the meat to the other plowmen, and they all had a great feast. Then he went with Elijah, as his assistant.

Elijah had a good reason for acting as he did toward Elisha. He was testing the genuineness of Elisha's vocation. This act of throwing his mantle or coat over Elisha was a language of behavior men understood in that day. It spoke of adoption. Just as fathers clothe their children, so Elijah would take Elisha under his personal care to bring him up in the things of God. Elisha recognized the full significance of this act. Immediately he responded by severing connections with his family and the occupation of farming. Elijah tried to discourage him. He asked him, as if he knew nothing of what he had done, "Why all the fuss, there is no need for change in your life?"

But genuine God-given vocation had been communicated. Elisha could answer with a sureness born of knowledge God alone plants in the heart. "I am coming because I am responding to a call from God to work in the ministry."

I have found that if I can discourage a man from pursuing the ministry, his call is not genuine. If he can be turned back by my words, what would he do under the pressure of real opposition on the field. This has proved a helpful means of sorting out those genuinely called from those who just have "ideas" about the ministry.

When God has called us we are so sure down inside that no one and nothing can keep us from following God's orders.

Called Pastor-Shepherds Demonstrate Commitment

Knowledge of God's calling grows within us. It consumes more and more of our thoughts and plans. We find ourselves setting lesser goals aside in order to give ourselves more completely to fulfilling that calling. This kind of commitment is worked in us by the Holy Spirit. He makes God's desires for us our consuming drive and passion. After a time we find that nothing else matters but our calling. This is not something we work up ourselves, but it is our response of investment to God's initiative in calling us.

As we look at Elisha after a number of years' service to Elijah, we find that his knowledge has grown into commitment. He cannot be deterred from fulfilling God's purpose for him. As Elijah's time of departure draws nigh, we find Elisha experiencing a series of tests of his commitment. Everyone, including fellow ministers and his own tutor tells him to forget it. Be satisfied with what you have. Do not persevere for fulfillment. But inside of Elisha's heart was a consuming passion and a dogged steadfastness which was similar to the Apostle Paul's when he said:

> Not as though I had already attained, either were already

> perfect: but I follow after, if that I may apprehend that for which also I am apprehended of Christ Jesus. Brethren, I count not myself to have apprehended: but this one thing I do, forgetting those things which are behind, and reaching forth unto those things which are before, I press toward the mark for the prize of the high calling of God in Christ Jesus. (Phil. 3:12-14)

The story of Elisha's preparation for taking over Elijah's position in 2 Kings 2 illustrates the drive to fulfill God's call that Paul so ably put into words in Philippians 3. If we do not have the sense of "this must be" inside, then we are not being bidden by the ascended Christ to feed His sheep. Genuine vocation cannot be denied. If we have heard His call, this will be seen in the total investment of our life to answer it. No cost of preparation will seem too great a sacrifice if we are responding to God. If the idea of ministering was our own or someone else's for us, we will find ourselves in the position of a hireling. When the pressure is on, we will quit.

Called Pastor-Shepherds Possess Faith And Patience

When we hear God speak, this creates faith. That is what a genuine word from God always does. When we have truly heard, we respond by believing and acting in obedience. The same faith that hears the call and sees the vision also sustains and holds us steady in patience. Vocation is a process and it does not happen overnight. Years and years of preparation in the school of the Holy Spirit are required. God will send into our life those things that will make us what God has called us to be. We are called "to be" an apostle, or a pastor-shepherd, or whatever. But we must grow up into Him before this becomes an actuality. This means passing the hardest test of all—the test of time.

I think waiting is one of the hardest things God ever asks us to do. But there are no shortcuts to fulfillment in ministry. I have never liked to wait. I can remember when I was a boy that one of the things I hated to hear my parents say was, "Wait. We'll think about it for a while." When I wanted a bicycle, I wanted it right then. I didn't want to wait. Every kid on the block had one; why did I have to "wait"? As we grow up to fulfill our vocation, we find that God waits to be gracious to us.

It is absolutely essential that faith and patience be developed in the pastor-shepherd. This is not only his means for inheriting the promises, but it is a qualification for attracting and keeping followers. People simply will not gather around and stick with a man who is always talking about things but never carries them through to fruition. We are commanded to seek out leaders who have passed this test of time. The writer to the Hebrews says:

> And we desire that everyone of you do shew the same diligence to the full assurance of hope unto the end: That ye be not slothful, but followers of them who through faith and patience inherit the promises. (6:11-12)

It is important that pastor-shepherds carry out the visions they have shared with the people. Sheep scatter quickly when they find that after they have given money for building projects, nothing is ever completed. Leaders must have the faith and patience to complete what they begin in God. It is better to undertake projects within the reach of the leader's faith and carry these out than to talk big and never build anything.

Called Pastor-Shepherds Act With Confidence

With genuine vocation comes a deep settled sureness. We can afford to relax about the work of God. We can be gentle with others. We can make room for others who demonstrate giftedness from God. I have learned that confidence is absolutely essential to success in life. When I play golf with my brother and some of the men from the church, I find that hanging loose is vital. When one of my opponents is trailing by a few strokes, I sometimes take advantage of his natural reaction of nervousness. I kid him, "Do you always stand that way? Do you always hold the club that way?" When we begin to press, it is all over. This is as true in the ministry as it is in sports.

Have you ever noticed that a novice usually tries too hard? He doesn't allow himself or others to make mistakes. He doesn't know how to be flexible. He is usually demanding and arbitrary. He is threatened by the giftedness in others and becomes competitive instead of being grateful for help. But the man who knows who he is in God, whose vocation is certain, can afford to be relaxed, to be simple, and enjoy life. When we have confidence, life is no longer a strain.

The confidence that results from a genuine pastoral vocation consists primarily of a clear-cut self-image, an identity as a man of destiny to serve God by helping people. This knowledge of who one is in God frees the pastor-shepherd from the many psychological games most people play in the attempt to be someone other than they are. The called pastor-shepherd has no need to project any image beyond what he really is in God. He can afford to be himself even when preaching or counseling with his people. The matter of identity has been solved through his vital union with the Chief Shepherd. This frees the pastor-shepherd's emotional energies from defensiveness and self-protection, allowing him margin to really care about others.

CHAPTER 18

The Voice of the Pastor—Shepherd

In John 10, we find several clear-cut comparisons between those men and women who were called by God to feed His sheep and those who appointed themselves to take what they can get by fleecing God's people.

SHEPHERD	HIRELING
(1) enters by the door; is recognized by the porter as legitimate	climbs up "some other way"
(2) the sheep know his voice	the sheep do not know his voice, but consider him a "stranger"
(3) calls his own sheep by name and leads them out	drives the sheep; cannot call them by name
(4) sheep follow him	sheep flee from him.
(5) will give his life if necessary to defend the sheep in danger	leaves the sheep in danger; more concerned about saving his own life
(6) cares for the sheep	concerned only for his own wages

Jesus gave these comparisons to help the people of His day sort out between who was really leading them into God and those who were taking advantage of them. He contrasted His own ministry with those who pretended to be leaders and "shepherds" but were in fact serving their own ends. But these same basic contrasts are just as valid today when we seek to distinguish those servants of God who are co-workers with Him from people who have put themselves into the ministry in order to seek their own pleasure.

All of these attributes find expression in the pastor-shepherd's voice. It is by His voice that he calls the sheep to follow him. The sheep instinctively know by the ring of that voice whether or not to respond to that call. The pastor-shepherd with a charisma from God has a voice that attracts sheep. This is something that no hireling can imitate.

The difference between the hireling and the genuine pastor-shepherd is a matter of relationship to the Great Shepherd. The voice of the genuine pastor-shepherd attracts sheep because it carries the same tones of genuine love and care that Christ has for each of His own. The pastor-shepherd is so vitally joined in personal union to the Great Shepherd that in a real sense the sheep are his own. He is no longer worried about wages, but this concern is that none of the sheep be lost. This kind of union with Christ results in great fruitfulness in pastoral ministry.

How Many Sheep Can A Pastor-Shepherd Handle?

Some teachers contend that since Jesus limited Himself to twelve disciples, we should not attempt to feed thousands. But Jesus' work with the twelve disciples was different from His work with the many sheep God gave to Him. These twelve were to lay the foundations for the church in apostolic doctrine and example.

Thousands thronged to hear Jesus. When Jesus told the parable of the lost sheep, He spoke of the shepherd having a hundred sheep. But it was not at all uncommon for the shepherds of those days to have several hundred sheep or even a few thousand. They often had several assistants and they used many dogs, but there was only one shepherd. Jesus saw the multitude as sheep, not the twelve.

> But when he saw the multitudes, he was moved with compassion on them, because they fainted, and were scattered abroad, as sheep having no shepherd. (Matt. 9:36)

Some say that after a church reaches about two hundred we need to divide it into smaller branches. But they fail to examine the examples in the New Testament. Early in the history of the Jerusalem church, it numbered over 8,120. At first people were "added" daily, but later on, as God's work through His people accelerated, believers were "multiplied." The number of people in a local church depends upon how many the pastor-shepherd can feed with his voice. For how many sheep can he share the Lord's burden of compassion? This varies with the man. We cannot set an arbitrary limit.

You don't know how many people you can handle until you begin feeding. But more important, it is not a question of limiting the number in the flock, but of the pastor-shepherd's personality expanding. As pastor-shepherds become more open to God and to people, the charisma becomes more apparent. More sheep hear and respond to his voice. We are not talking about eloquence, but about the power to gather and feed people.

Pastor-shepherds differ in gathering capacity. Some pastor-shepherds attract only a few sheep during a lifetime; others attract many thousands. This is a matter of difference in gift. God only requires us to be fruitful according to the capacity He has given us. Nor is it entirely a matter of more prayer. Many times people are offended by lack of personal discipline. Poor grooming, tardiness, carelessness about keeping promises, overeating—any of these little foxes can spoil the fruitfulness of an entire pastoral ministry. We are responsible to cultivate the gift God has deposited within us to its full potential.

During the two centuries immediately after the writing of the New Testament, confusion entered into the church about the authority of the pastor-shepherd as a charismatic leader. It was assumed that because he settled down to tend one flock instead of traveling like the apostles and prophets, he must be uninspired and inferior to them.

J.A. Robinson comments about this departure from New Testament pattern:

> To say that the local ministry was local is a harmless remark; but to imply that the local ministry was not a gift of God to the whole Church, so to depreciate it in comparison with the prophets and other teachers, who sprang up within the bosom of the local community, but might be recognized for their gifts in other communities which they chose to visit—this is to go beyond anything the New Testament gives any hint. The implication is directly mischievous when it leads on to the conclusion that Prophets and Teachers were persons of authority, who had a right to address local communities in the name of the Church as a whole. (*The Primitive Ministry*, p. 77)

As charisma declined, authority had to be gained in other ways. For this reason, ideas of ecclesiastical hierarchy came to be exaggerated. The term bishop was separated from the other terms applied to the pastor-shepherd and made into an office of greater importance. Instead of being the gifted presiding elder of the local community, the bishop was elevated to oversee not one, but several churches. Organization by men replaced rule by God.

The Pastor-Shepherd's Voice Is Reassuring

Something within each one of us as God's sheep cries for the security of being under the care of one who knows what he is doing and who does it with the firmness born of confidence. This need for the reassurance which comes from authority is as obvious in natural sheep as it is in God's people. Take, for example, this illustration:

> During an early night watch I once visited a shepherd in his sheepfold; and hearing him occasionally call out

> "Hoo! Ha! Ha!" I asked, "Is it necessary to call out thus during the night?" He answered: "My dear boy, if I don't call out to my sheep thus, they will hear the voice of their enemies, and be frightened. If they do not hear my voice, they will hear the prowling of the wolves as they come nearer and nearer to the fold. They need to hear my voice in order that they may enjoy a quiet and restful sleep." (*The Shepherd Song on the Hills of Lebanon*, p. 36)

In this same way, our American cowboys sang to their cattle. Many of our Western songs are actually addressed to cows. Even the rasping voice of the singing cowboy kept the cattle peaceable and less likely to stampede.

An Oriental shepherd observed the similarity between natural sheep and God's people. Both have a deep need for periodic reminders that they are of personal value to the shepherd. Both thrive on his periodic touches of intimate concern and tender affection. Let's hear it in his own descriptive language:

> When the sheep are put forth in the morning each takes his place, like a disciplined army, in the grazing line, and keeps the same position throughout the day. When tending my sheep I wondered much at this. Once during the day each sheep would break away from the line and approaching the shepherd with an expectant eye, lift a mild "baa" or "huh huh." The shepherds know the meaning of this . . . the shepherd by holding out his hand encourages the sheep and the sheep runs to him. The shepherd then rubs its nose and ears, scratches its chin, strokes his hand over its back with a few gentle taps on the shoulder, whispers love words into its ears, "How do you like your shepherd? Did you enjoy your food today? Any briars or thorns, or snake bites?" And he fondles it affectionately. The sheep, in the meantime, rubs against the shepherd's leg, telling him with all its

> strength that it loves him, or, if the shepherd be sitting down, nibbles at his ears, the ears that are ever open to its cry, and rubs its cheek like a true lover against the face of the faithful herder. After a few moments of such communion and exchange of love and friendship with the master, and finding fulness of joy in his presence, the sheep returns to its place in the feeding line refreshed and made content by the personal contact with the shepherd. (*The Spirit of the Shepherd*, p. 59)

Pastoral counseling is often the best route to solving personal and family problems. And these times of individual attention enhance the times of public ministry. I learned from these sessions what problems are common among the people at any given time. In hearing from God about one such problem, I often find I can preach to the whole congregation and meet many such problems in one service. But more important, they begin to listen with increased confidence to the entire counsel of God's word, having learned in one small personal experience that His wisdom exceeds ours.

We must be careful, however, to preserve a balance between time spent in individual counseling and time spent feeding the flock as a whole. Some people seem to need a private pastor all their own. They do not want the responsibility of making their own decisions.

A Voice Within A Voice

This phenomenon of the voice within the voice, the inspired word, makes all the difference between dead letter and life. There are two Greek words that are often translated "word" in our English Bibles. One of these is *logos*. It speaks of eternal principle.

The second is *rhema*. This term refers to a statement on a specific occasion. This *rhema* is "now" in contrast to the "forever" of the *logos*. God has declared himself in finality as the *logos*, the unchanging. But He also periodically speaks to us a *rhema*, or personal word appropriate to a particular situation. It is about this kind of living word that Jesus said:

> It is the spirit that quickeneth; the flesh profiteth nothing: the words that I speak unto you, they are spirit, and they are life. (John 6:63)

God is sanctifying, cleansing, and washing the church by the living word that proceeds out of His mouth—the *rhema* (Eph. 5:26). For many years people heard only the *logos* in some general and impersonal way; they did not know they could hear the fresh and living word applied both directly by the Holy Spirit and through the anointed word of a minister. And people are excited about this.

But in any kind of excitement we must always be careful that we do not lose our balance. There is no *rhema* that does not agree with the *logos*. This is a test that must be applied to anything we claim to have heard from God whether directly or through one of His servants. God never contradicts himself. The Spirit and the word agree.

Since there is the possibility of error, God has given us safeguards. We can judge these words. We can see what actually comes to pass. We can check all that is spoken against what has already been written by the inspiration of the Spirit in Scripture.

Probably the most important safeguard in this matter of hearing fresh direction from God is the local church. Here we have a sounding board for any prophecy or revelation we might feel we have. We can express it openly and have others with proven ministries judge what we have to say. But we must beware of the feeling that we have a revelation for the entire body of Christ.

I don't think any of us have a right to impose teaching on the entire body of Christ until it is a working principle in a local situation. God intended the local church to provide a sort of "seed plot" where we can try our revelations and direction. Then when it produces results others will see the grace of God among us and become open to receiving the same revelation. Influence from one local church to another is spiritual. We do learn from one another, but we learn what not to do as well as what to do.

National and international ministers have no scriptural warrant for seeking to influence others on a wide basis without a local seed plot which can be investigated. If you are teaching it, show it to me in practical terms, in flesh and blood people. If you cannot provide practical demonstration, you are theorizing. Theorizing is extremely dangerous. We must know what we are doing. We must see how the *rhema* fits with the *logos* and how it works in real life.

We are pastor-shepherds in local situations. We have our hands full with the local church. My voice can influence you spiritually, but I cannot influence you arbitrarily.

CHAPTER 19

Restoring Pastoral Charisma

No greater blessing can come to the church than a visitation by the Holy Spirit. Unfortunately, some of the clergy do not understand the fresh winds of the Spirit. Instead of welcoming such a visitation, they have become threatened. Their people run off to prayer meetings and businessmen's breakfasts, and even to large conventions in other cities, where they mix with sheep from many kinds of folds. "What can this bring but confusion?" they say.

But, in actuality, the charismatic visitation means not only that his people will be revitalized and given a fresh hunger for God's word, but that his own pastoral charisma will be restored. Pastor-shepherd will cease being an office and become once more the ministry given by the ascended Christ. Those who have been baptized into the Lordship of Christ will be able to obey genuine pastoral authority.

Those who study church growth have been saying for years that the people are hungry for authority. Rapidly growing churches have been described as conservative in doctrine and strict in discipline. Pastor-shepherds, it is time for you to arise and put on your God-given mantle. Be clothed with the authority God has given you and the sheep will flock to you in unbelievable numbers.

God Has A Pattern

God's pattern has always been to have a shepherd rule by feeding, gathering, carrying, and leading. A shepherd may have many assistants and many dogs, but there is only one shepherd at the head of the flock.

Moses cried to God during a time of leadership crisis, and God responded by providing seventy assistants, or elders.

> And the LORD said unto Moses, Gather unto me seventy men of the elders of Israel, whom thou knowest to be the elders of the people, and officers over them; and bring them unto the tabernacle of the congregation, that they may stand there with thee. And I will come down and talk with thee there: and I will take of the spirit which is upon thee, and will put it upon them; and they shall bear the burden of the people with thee, that thou bear it not thyself alone. (Num. 11:16-17)

Not only must the pastor-shepherd have charisma to gather sheep, but to gather other able leaders around him. This is a much neglected aspect of the pastor-shepherd's oversight. But, if the pastor-shepherd is not functioning in the power of God, other ministries cannot function properly. How can the teacher teach until the pastor-shepherd has gathered people into one place? To whom can the prophet prophesy but the gathered flock?

When, however, Moses was close to death, God did not set Moses' mantle on the shoulders of the seventy. He recognized instead a basic need for one leader. God answered Moses' last prayer by raising up another man to take his place, Joshua.

> And the Lord said unto Moses, Take thee Joshua the son of Nun, a man in whom is the spirit, and lay thine hand upon him; and set him before Eleazar the priest, and before all the congregation; and give him a charge in their sight. And thou shalt put some of thine honour upon

> him, that all the congregation of the children of Israel may be obedient. And he shall stand before Eleazar the priest, who shall ask counsel for him after the judgment of Urim before the LORD: at his word shall they go out, and at his word they shall come in, both he, and all the children of Israel with him, even all the congregation. (Num. 27:18-21)

Several important aspects of the pastor-shepherd's ministry are brought out in this passage.

(1) God directs in the selection of one leader to be set over the entire congregation, including its elders.

(2) This leader must be recognized publicly. In this way the people will know to give him their allegiance.

(3) The obedience of the people is a spontaneous spiritual response to the gift of government in the appointed leader.

(4) The pastor-shepherd has the initiative; at his word people come and go.

(5) As the pastor-shepherd progresses in his walk before the Lord, the people go with him. His ability to gather means that the people want to stay with him wherever he goes in his pursuit of God's goals for the community.

The best way to measure the gift of government is by looking at the response of the followers. When God plants a leader, his ministry will in time prove fruitful.

Three pictures of the church will help us understand the nature of its leadership: the church as God's family, the church as God's army, and the church as the body of Christ. We will begin by comparing the ministry of the pastor-shepherd with the function of the father in a family.

The Church As God's Family

Most of us agree that a good father will not only provide for his family, but will also discipline them, protect them, and be an example. The pastor-shepherd cares for his sheep like a father of a family because God gives him grace to fulfill his calling.

If a father does not support his family and feed them as he should, he will come to disgrace and possibly face divorce proceedings. The man who pastors the flock of God must likewise have spiritual food for the people.

The Apostle Paul emphasized that a bishop must maintain order and discipline of his own household before he could take responsibility for the church (1 Tim. 3:4-5). The New Testament bishop or pastor-shepherd was to be the leader of one congregation. He was to look after them just as a father cares for his family.

The Church As God's Army

The second picture of the church that will help us understand pastoral leadership is that of an army. The gift of the Holy Spirit does much more than bless us with joy and new spiritual understanding. It changes us. It creates within our rebellious hearts the capacity to submit to authority. The Psalmist prophesied: "Thy people shall be willing in the day of thy power" (Psa. 110:3).

Those who belong to God through election will come to Him of their own volition (cf. John 6:37). But the idea is not only one of volunteering but of spontaneous delight.

Rebels are transformed into volunteers through the power of the ascended Christ. And Christ takes these volunteers and gives them to His church. The five ascension ministries are men and women who had first become freewill offerings to Christ. When He gave them to the church, this spirit of self-giving became contagious. Others gave themselves, and many were added to the Lord.

When we are in an army, we forget about our petty differences and all work toward the common goal of victory. We lay aside our differences and work shoulder to shoulder because each one of us is responding to something larger than our own concerns.

The Church As The Body Of Christ

The third image of the church—the body of Christ—will further help us understand the pastor's true function. It underlines our interdependence, relatedness, and communication. Since Christ can move directly upon and within each member of His church through the Holy Spirit, why do we find a visible structure of authority in each local church?

The church is structured in the same way the human body is structured—to provide a framework for complex life. In the field of biology, distinction and order among the cells of more complex organisms make them different from organisms composed of only one or a few cells which all perform the same basic tasks. But in more complex organisms, these functions are separated. Cells become specialists in one of these tasks, such as breathing, elimination, or digestion. Those cells having like functions group together to form organs; the organs in turn form systems to carry out these specialized tasks. Specialization makes for greater versatility in and capacity for life, as long as the various parts are coordinated.

To insure proper coordination among the parts, some cells and organs must specialize in leadership. In the human body this task is handled by the central nervous system. Leadership specialists are no less essential to the body of Christ.

CHAPTER 20

The Joy of Sheep-shearing Time

Sheep provide several different forms of wealth. Among them are meat, milk, leather, and fertilizer (from their bones). Rams' horns were used as containers for oil and as trumpets. In addition, sheep were commonly employed in the system of animal sacrifices of the Old Testament.

But by far the most important product of sheep is wool. When sheep were domesticated, men crossbred them to refine their wool. Not all sheep produce the same kind of wool, and even among sheep of the same breed, other factors, such as diet, determine the quality of the wool.

Sheep Need To Be Shorn

Sheep are shorn immediately after lambing time in the spring. Shepherds celebrate the event by calling their families and friends to a great feast. It was a time for dancing and rejoicing which often lasted for over a week.

Sheep instinctively resist shearing. For this reason, the shepherd must tie the sheep's front legs to prevent it from jumping about. Oddly enough, sheep do not make any sound while being sheared. This is why Isaiah said of the Christ, ". . . and as a sheep before her shearers is dumb, so he openeth not his mouth" (53:7).

Sheep should be sheared. This is not a cruel act, because unshorn sheep soon become a problem to themselves. The wool grows down over their eyes until they can no longer see. It becomes so heavy that they easily become cast. Wool collects quantities of mud and briars. Insects and tics love to nestle in it. Shearing sheep does them a real service.

Tithing Is A Law Of Blessing

The shearing of sheep pictures the reciprocal relationship which must exist between God's people and their pastor-shepherd. They too must be shorn or they will suffer consequences. People were designed to tithe and to give offerings as sheep were meant to produce wool. To deny people the opportunity to support the ministry of those who tend them is as cruel as allowing the wool to blind and weigh down natural sheep. They need to give.

The tithe is the first tenth of our income—even before the taxes and other expenses are subtracted. The tithe already belongs to God and to withhold it from Him is to rob Him (Mal. 3:8-12).

But as we give, God gives back to us, not only in material ways but in happiness and spiritual well-being. Prosperity always accompanies generosity. In the Proverbs we read: "There is that scattereth, and yet increaseth; and there is that withholdeth more than is meet, but it tendeth to poverty. The liberal soul shall be made fat: and he that watereth shall be watered also himself" (11:24-25).

Giving enables us to master our material temptations. Failure to keep material gain subordinate to the kingdom of His goals makes us unable to remain loyal in our love for the Great Shepherd. Our wool can get in the road of spiritual progress.

As sheep we must receive our periodic shearings. We must give in proportion to our increase.

Just as a river will become a swamp if it cannot flow, so our lives will become a reeking swamp if we do not let the benefits God sends us flow on to others. Luke puts it this way: "Give, and it shall be given unto you; good measure, pressed down, and shaken together, and running over, shall men give into your bosom. For with the same measure that ye mete withal it shall be measured to you again" (6:38).

Nothing blinds a man to the person he really is like money. Jesus said that it is easier for a camel to go through the eye of a needle than for a rich man to get into the kingdom. A man with money almost inevitably has an inflated opinion of himself. After all, he is self-sufficient. It is nearly impossible to see himself as needy or helpless. The wool has been pulled over his eyes.

One of the greatest services a pastor-shepherd can render to a rich man is to cut away this excessive wool and get it operating in the marketplace of the kingdom. Tithing lays up treasures in heaven. It is like putting your money into a Swiss bank account.

The sheared wool belongs to the shepherd who has tended the sheep. In the same way the tithe should go to the local church under supervision of the pastor.

This is a part of the law of blessing. If we bless those who feed us God's word, they will be freed from financial concerns to give themselves to the task of shepherding us. "Let him who is taught the word share all good things with him who teaches" (Gal. 6:6, RSV).

The quality and quantity of the wool is directly related to the pasturage and general health of the sheep. The wise shepherd knows to choose the finest of pasturage for his flock if he wants a good harvest of wool. Feeding and tending sheep in such a way that they will produce up to their full capacity is a task requiring skill and wisdom. Likewise for the pastor-shepherd, finding balance is never easy, and maintaining it for a group of people is all the more difficult. The man or woman who succeeds at it is certainly worthy of his or her hire.

There is a clear connection between government and finances. When we give tribute to a Caesar, we acknowledge his authority to rule over us. It is the duty of rulers to assess their people according to the needs of their nations.

Throughout the Bible we find the flow of wealth from God's people to His delegated authorities who in turn use the funds to support themselves. Most of the animal sacrifices, for example, were to be eaten by the priests.

In the Old Testament tithing began before the institution of the law. Abraham gave tithes to Melchizedek, who had blessed him in the name of God the maker of heaven and earth and the source of all his increase (Gen. 14:18-20). Jacob probably learned of the tithe from his grandfather and father, for we find him vowing a tenth to God when in a tight spot (Gen. 28:20-22).

But the law of Moses made everything about God's requirements more clear-cut than they had been in patriarchal days. God wanted to show men their own distaste for His rule over them. The law exposes human rebellion against authority and prepares men to accept a savior from the inner corruption of sin. The law said that giving was to be proportional, according to what men had received. It was to be given to the priests and Levites, who used it to maintain themselves and tend the tabernacle.

In the New Testament, the tithes and offerings were brought into the local church. At first the apostles made the decisions as to how to use the money. But as the various local assemblies matured and developed local ministries, the pastor-shepherd and his elders determined what to do with the money. The New Testament gives no warrant for one local church tithing to another or to any outside headquarters. Finances flowed from one church to another in the form of freewill offerings, as in the case of the relief fund Paul collected from the Gentile churches to help the Jerusalem church.

Whoever controls the church's finances ultimately controls the church. Funds must be put into the hands of God's appointed leaders. When this doesn't happen, role-confusion and conflicts arise and leadership is paralyzed. The pastor-shepherd must have the right of initiative in deciding what to do with the church funds and when to do it. Without this power he has no practical authority. He must not do it by coercion, but by inspiring confidence which will cause all to want to work with him for the welfare of the entire flock.

CHAPTER 21

Gathering or Scattering?

What makes a pastor-shepherd attractive to people? The Bible is full of examples of men who drew others after them in love for God: Moses, Joshua, David, Peter, Barnabas, Paul, James the Lord's brother, and John, to mention only a few. But there were others who mightily proclaimed God's truth but had no personal following: Elijah, Elisha, Jeremiah, Ezekiel and Apollos among them. What made the difference?

Charles Haddon Spurgeon gathered sheep by the thousands in nineteenth-century London. He offered his own explanation for his success.

> Love is the chief endowment for a pastor; you *must* love Christ if you mean to serve him in the capacity of pastor. Our Lord deals with the most vital point. The question is not "Simon, son of Jonas, knowest thou me?" though that would not have been an unreasonable question, since Peter had said, "I know not the man." He might have asked, "Simon, son of Jonas, knowest thou the deep mysteries of God?" He did know them, for his Lord had called him blessed for knowing that which flesh and blood had not revealed to him. Our great

> Bishop of souls did not examine him with regard to his mental endowments, nor upon his other spiritual qualification, but only upon this one, "Simon, son of Jonas, lovest thou me? If so, then, Feed my sheep." Does not this plainly show us that the chief endowment of the pastor is to love Christ supremely; only such a man as that is fit to look after Christ's sheep. You will fulfill that office well if you love Jesus: your love will keep you in your Lord's company, it will hold you under his immediate supervision, and will secure you his help. Love to him will breed a love for all his sheep, and your love for them will give you power over them. Experience testifies that we never gain a particle of power for good over our people by angry words, but we obtain an almost absolute power over them by all-enduring love; indeed, the only power which it is desirable for us to have must come in that way. I have had the high pleasure of loving some of the most objectionable people till they loved me; and some of the most bitter I have altogether won by refusing to be displeased, and by persisting in believing that they could do better. (*Spurgeon's Expository Encyclopedia*, vol. II, p. 80)

Spurgeon spoke of what he knew. But love is not the difference between the man who gathers sheep and the man who declares prophetic truth in self-sacrificing faithfulness, for both have love. The difference is not in devotion, but in the gifts and callings of God.

Some men preach eloquently. They have us on the edges of our seats as they unfold the depth and wealth of God's message to His church. What an anointing these men have! But very often they are men who are not suited to close involvement with people. They frequently ask me not to give out their phone number or the name of the motel where they are staying.

I have watched some of these men attempt to pastor a local church. Invariably they have a strong beginning, but within a few months or a year they dwindle to nothing. Their power to preach is undiminished but the sheep were not satisfied with eloquence and revelation alone. These mighty men of the word are called to itinerant ministry. God divides the gifts severally as He wills.

We who are called to be pastors must learn how to cooperate with the Holy Spirit if the gifts of God are to operate effectively through us. Some things are only learned by experience. There are reasons why sheep come together and thrive under the ministry of one, and quickly disperse when another attempts to pastor them.

How to Scatter Sheep

Twenty years ago I thought one of the things that would build a church quickly and solidly was an emphasis on the miraculous. I was sure that if I could get God to perform enough miracles, the people would come in droves.

But I have since learned that God does not build a church so much by signs and wonders as by the teaching of His word. Miracles excite the sheep. But in the long run only the word of God enables believers to grow and multiply.

Emphasizing miracles has a built-in limit. The first night, God heals a woman who is blind. She runs around shouting, "I can see! I can see!" Everyone is thrilled. The next night the people expect more of the same. It is not enough to have the blind see. What about the deaf and the lame? So, the second night God enables a man to walk who was formerly paralyzed. He jumps off his stretcher and prances around the platform. The people go wild with excitement. But they always want more, especially if it's sensational. What do we do the third night, raise the dead? And even if the dead were raised it wouldn't feed the sheep.

Charismatics especially need to guard against becoming miracle-oriented. Often they are people who were sitting in cold and dry churches hearing what God used to do. Then they discovered for themselves that God still heals. But miracles, signs, wonders, and gifts of the Spirit were given to confirm the message of the word. Their purpose is to authenticate the gospel. They were never intended to replace preaching and teaching, but to support it.

Another way to scatter sheep is to give them too much responsibility too soon. Among literal shepherds this is known as "overdriving the flock." Pushing the sheep too fast or too far can kill the lambs and the weaker sheep, and, in time, the entire flock. The same kind of thing happens in the local church. A pastor can overdrive his flock by pushing it too rapidly into teaching beyond its depth.

The Bible makes a distinction between the "milk" and "meat" of the word for good reason. Beginners must be fed milk until they have become grounded in Christ. If we try to go on without making sure our spiritual foundations are correctly laid, it will catch up with us later, usually at an embarrassing moment.

Some years back we had to expand our educational facilities. A four-story building would join hard to the sanctuary. Excavations began. In a few days the architect and building contractor called us together for a meeting. The west wall of the sanctuary, they told us, would have to be underpinned—it didn't have a proper foundation. If we added any more weight, it would collapse. It would cost us a little over $40,000 to make it right. At that moment, we realized the value of proper foundations. And so we have learned to pasture the flock of Bethesda in the green grass of the basics of Christian doctrine for as long as is needed. We have disciplined ourselves to avoid the sensational in favor of the nutritional.

The Bethesda Missionary Temple specializes in preparing people to serve others in whatever ways God chooses. In fact, we believe God has shown us that we are an "armory" because He wants us to equip people to function according to His calling. But again I had to learn not to overdrive the flock.

I thought that if each person in the local church experienced the laying on of hands and prophecy, and had a direct revelation of his or her ministry, everything would flow together. We would have a strong and active local church. But soon I discovered that this was not the Lord's plan for us.

Instead of motivating people to become overcomers and equipping them for service, this practice paralyzed them with confusion, fear, and self-consciousness. They stopped the things they were already doing. They did not know what to do with all their revelations about the future. It was more than they could handle.

Another way in which we can overdrive the sheep is by too much activity. We once thought that the more meetings people could attend when God was moving and truth was flowing, the more quickly they would grow. Surely you could not get too much good preaching and worship. So it would seem. People need time to digest what they have gained from seasons of revelation and instruction. They need to apply it and test it in everyday life. It is possible to become overstuffed and get too little exercise.

In 1949 we experienced a tremendous outpouring of the Holy Spirit as did many other places. God was moving in fresh dimensions. Preaching was easy. Worship flowed. Anything could happen. People flowed into our meetings from everywhere—literally from the north, south, east, and west.

Since the people were from such diverse backgrounds, we thought the sheepfold might expand more easily if we dispensed with divisive doctrines. This was not a time to haggle about the Lord's Supper, or church government, or eschatology. This was a time to love everybody and embrace all who wanted to become a part of things—or so we reasoned.

We almost dispensed with water baptism. We were so free that anyone could be baptized any way he wished—or not at all. We wanted everyone to feel comfortable and welcome. Away with teaching that would categorize people!

But after a few years of blessing, these people who had begun so well started to fall backwards. Some lost interest for one reason or another and simply dropped out of the active ranks. Others became confused and went off into doctrinal by-paths. We had failed the sheep by refusing to set high standards and by neglecting to lay foundational truths in their lives. God called us to repentance. We leaders would have to return to God's priorities.

The immediate result of our change of attitude about doctrine and discipline was devastating. Church attendance dropped. But as we persisted in faithfulness to what we believed God was telling us, growth returned. The sheep who began to come after that remained with us steadily. They were no longer blown about by every wind of doctrine. Fads held little appeal for them. Instead we saw, growing up before our eyes, healthy sheep with good wool that grew back year after year.

Any dietary imbalance will in time produce a loss of appetite. You simply cannot eat steak every day and retain a relish for it. The same is true with any gift of the Holy Spirit if it is overemphasized. I have attended churches where in every meeting there will be four or five prophetic utterances. After a day or two of this, you no longer listen. Instead you grow weary and hope the leader will direct the service along another avenue. We can't sort out the good from the bad. Consequently, we tend to discard it all. A prophetic message given at the right time is tremendously edifying, but too much has the tendency to produce the opposite effect.

How to Gather Sheep

We have examined several practices which scatter God's sheep. But experience has taught us that certain procedures gather God's people. I have already mentioned some of them. They often seemed doomed to failure and sure to bring division, but turned out to be means for great blessing. When my sister Pat first proposed to instruct our church children in basic Bible truths by means of a catechism, I was sure we would be taking a turn for the worse. The word "catechism" had a strange feel. I had always associated it with Catholics, Lutherans, and other liturgical groups. But as we looked into the meaning of the word, we discovered that it described an old and reliable method of teaching—as old as the church itself. It uses a series of questions and answers to instill doctrine in an orderly and sensible fashion. And its use among us has brought great blessing to our church and given us a heightened sense of unity.

Doctrine, after all, is simply systematic teaching from the Bible. When we prepare the food well, the sheep eat it, retain it, and grow. But all doctrine must be related to the person of Christ. Apart from His presence and the enlivening work of the Holy Spirit, doctrine will become a dead letter.

The presence of Jesus Christ in a worship service is that indefinable something that gathers the sheep. Every born-again Christian should be able to discern the presence of God's Spirit, even though he might not be able to articulate exactly what he feels. But, once he has felt it, he'll notice it strongly when it is absent. If the lack of His presence continues in the local church and the congregation is one that has become spiritually aware, it is only a matter of time until they will go elsewhere to find the presence they are seeking.

But let me make it clear that we have not tried to build our unity on doctrine, but on the Spirit. No matter how hard we try there will never be a time this side of heaven when everyone in the church agrees completely on all matters of doctrine. That has taught us to accept people as they are and receive them as Christ receives us. As we all relax in the Spirit of God, He will blend us together into genuine *koinonia*.

While my wife, Anne, and I were raising our three children, we had to learn to accept their immaturity at the same time that we were trying to help them grow out of it. We spoke to our kids when they couldn't understand one word we said. We taught them to talk, to sing, to appreciate beauty, to get involved with people, to keep house, to wash windows. We were loving and enjoying each other so that eventually we would be able to converse intelligibly as adults, loving and enjoying the same things.

This is the way it is in the family of God. We continue to love and share all we have received from the Lord with those around us, in hopes that eventually we will all feel the same way about the same things. We will be a genuine family, enjoying our Father, each other, and our accumulated knowledge.

Does God really intend for our relationships in the church to be as strong as those of a family? It would seem that He meant them to be even stronger (Matt. 12:46-50). The idea of the church as a covenant community is becoming a working principle.

The word "covenant" means "a binding agreement, a treaty, a pact." The blood of Jesus not only joins us to God but ties us to one another as "blood brothers." Covenant makes us into a family with a closeness and willingness to give to each other which supersedes even our natural kinship ties.

The problem with our American society is that our relationships have become superficial. We are acquainted with people, but we don't really know them. We work for the same company, but usually our commitment is to give our time for wages. If another company will pay us more, we will quickly make a shift with few emotional pangs or feelings of disloyalty.

Lifelong commitment to anybody or anything is rare in our society. This is a minus and not a plus. I have the feeling that there are certain people in my social circle who will need me around for the rest of their lives. This is what the family of God is all about. We supplement each other, not for a week, or a month, or a year, but through a lifetime. This is what ails so many of our youth. They have no one who really cares.

Jesus said, ''He that is not with me is against me: and he that gathereth not with me scattereth'' (Luke 11:23). That brings us full circle to the starting place of this chapter. We have looked at those practices that scatter and those that gather the sheep. And finally we looked briefly at one of the purposes God has in gathering us together in His family.

CHAPTER 22

God Initiates Change in Sheepfolds

God's people should not censure or criticize their leaders. They are to regard them as anointed by God and should not even touch them with derogatory words (1 Chron. 16:22). The Bible forbids open rebuke of leaders or the entertaining of any accusation made against them unless it is substantiated by reliable witnesses (1 Tim. 5:1, 19-20).

The sheep must be able to look to their leaders with profound respect, deep trust, and a desire to be like them. Without this, wholehearted obedience and submission are not possible. If we are to follow our leaders without reservation or hesitation, their example must be impeccable.

God himself initiates all judgment, including that of taking sheep from one undershepherd and assigning them to others. He may do this by removing the disqualified leader and scattering intervention. But never does God allow the sheep to take matters into their own hands.

If there has been a problem in one sheepfold, it cannot be avoided by moving down the street to another sheepfold. Local churches should communicate with each other. If a sheep leaves one sheepfold for another in order to escape discipline, the pastor-shepherd of the new sheepfold must know what the case is. Sometimes the matter in the former sheepfold must be resolved before the person can be received into fellowship in the new fold.

We carry our problems with us wherever we go. What we do not solve in the first place, will recur in the next place, and the next until we deal with the root of the problem. The source of our difficulties is within us rather than our situations. Sooner or later God insists that we recognize this in order that we may repent, be converted, and become different people. For this reason He requires His faithful pastor-shepherds to investigate the reasons sheep have left other folds and to deal with the sheep according to their real need.

Stay Under The Cloud

The Lord alone knows where the pasture is right for us. It is easy to think we are being led when in fact we are pursuing our own course. God "plants" us in the house of the Lord, and if we will submit to this we will flourish. This is what the Psalmist discovered:

> Those that he planted in the house of the LORD shall flourish in the courts of our God. They shall still bring forth fruit in old age; they shall be fat and flourishing. (92:13-14)

God's leadership means that we will follow purposes which are not our own. Peter was an impetuous man. Jesus told him that one day he would be carried where he did not want to go—on that day he would no longer be the impetuous, willful man he once had been. And, just so, Jesus calls us from our willfulness to be His servants, to give up our goals for His.

When Israel came out of the land of Egypt, God was taking them somewhere. They had a destiny. They were going to be a free people as never before. They had been a nation of slaves. Now they were going to be people of consequence, with whom the world must reckon—all of this because of God's leadership.

God was leading them to Canaan—only a matter of a few days'

journey across the Sinai Peninsula. But they wandered for forty years in the wilderness because they would not submit to leadership. The people who came out of Egypt—with the exception of Caleb and Joshua—never entered their inheritance. We don't want to become a wandering people because we fail to cooperate with God's leadership.

Guidance Is A Community Matter

We hear much talk today about guidance. But we are in danger of over-emphasizing personal guidance. We teach that the Holy Spirit should have free reign in our lives. The Bible tells us that those who are led by the Spirit are the sons of God.

But we dare not allow one Scripture to seem more important than other Scriptures on the same topic. We are not only guided by the Holy Spirit personally, but we are guided by the Holy Spirit through our leaders. God directs us through the decisions of our pastor-shepherd. This is an important matter when we are considering the possibility of leaving one fold for another.

Many people fail to recognize the community dimension of God's shepherding. They forget that God's sheep are in a flock. For them guidance is a private affair, between them and the Lord. They are missing the safety that is found in wise counsel. They can't believe that if they stay in a local church community, they will be led by God. But, too often, they have deceived themselves. What they really fear is that, if they submit to a pastor, he might oppose their willfulness.

Notice the way God led the nation of Israel. Wherever His cloud or pillar of fire went, they were to follow. It was that simple. But such guidance was not agreeable to the natural reasoning of these people. They would have preferred a map, a timetable—something concrete and predictable. The movement of the cloud and the pillar was erratic. They could not anticipate what He would do next. He did not tell them what their next stop would be. They were reduced to depending upon His presence.

When God leads, He leads for good reasons. But He often keeps those reasons to himself. The cloud protected the people in a situation where they could not survive without it. It may not be as obvious, but we are equally dependent upon God's presence. He may lead us into experiences and situations we would not choose for ourselves. But unless we stay under the blessing of His presence, we too will perish in the wilderness.

The cloud remained some places only a day or two, in others for a week, and still others for a month. Once in a while it remained in the same place for a year. Those must have been trying times for Israel. And what about us today? "I'm saved, I have the baptism in the Holy Spirit and the gifts of the Spirit; I'm going someplace fast—if somebody will just tell me where to go."

When we're going to Canaan, we don't want to sit in one place in the desert for a year. Day after day we look at the cloud, but it doesn't move. We chafe. We put pressure on other people because of our anxiety and distrust of God's leadership.

But the cloud remained in one place for a year because the people were not ready to go on. Moses could not lead the people forward until God's presence went before them. But the people did not understand God's good intentions. While they were under the cloud and experiencing supernatural provision they became irritable. Their anger grew into rebellion.

We do the same thing. We begin to feel as though we're not getting anywhere. But if we're in the presence of God, we are in a good spot. In time the cloud will move; not only for you personally, but for all of us as a community.

The cloud does not follow us. You cannot go anyplace you choose and expect to take God's presence and blessing with you. We all come to years of retirement and times of change. But these can be dangerous times. I have seen people retire and go to Florida, or California, or Arizona, sure that the cloud would be there. But it wasn't. That doesn't deny God's omnipresence, it only means that we must not take for granted that God will bless our choices. We need to move in obedience, not willfulness. The pattern of God's visitation is erratic. You cannot predict where you will find it.

I have seen pastor-shepherds make this same mistake. They experienced God's blessing in one place and assumed that they could carry this to the next place. They thought they carried the cloud around with them. But when they carried out their plans, they found out otherwise.

People frequently call us with requests for ministers. They say, "We have a group of people here who need pastoring. You have so many well-trained people there at Bethesda. Why don't you send somebody to help us?" But we cannot arbitrarily send people to places and expect the cloud to follow them. We must follow the cloud and that means we must wait for God's initiative.

Many people have asked me, "Don't you think you have spent enough time in Detroit?"

I answer them, "No, I'm not going anywhere. I'm going to stay under the cloud!"

CHAPTER 23

God's Discipline of Pastor-Shepherds

Field Marshal Montgomery has said, "The degree of [a leader's] influence will depend on the personality of the man, the 'incandescence' of which he is capable, the flame which burns within him, the magnetism which will draw the hearts of men towards him." He listed seven essential characteristics of a leader, which can be paraphrased as follows:

(1) He is objectively detached from detail.
(2) He avoids entanglement in petty reactions.
(3) He does not take himself too seriously.
(4) He knows how to pick good men to help him.
(5) He trusts his assistants enough to give them liberty to work.
(6) He can make clear and definite decisions.
(7) He inspires confidence.

These same qualities which distinguish natural leaders also mark the spiritually gifted leader. God does not pick someone and then override his natural potential and limitations, but stimulates and enhances the natural propensities for leadership already resident in the personality. Because this is the case, it is a common temptation for spiritual leaders to rely too much upon themselves. They begin to think of themselves too highly. Many times they expect their own charm and personality—their "way with people"—to accomplish what only the Spirit of God can do.

An equally dangerous temptation is the tendency to discount what one possesses naturally, in an unrealistic supposition that the Spirit will cause him to become everything he is not. But this is not how He works. He chooses to wed the spiritual and the natural, and make something out of us we could not be apart from Him.

J. Oswald Sanders states this principle well:

> Spiritual leadership is a blending of natural and spiritual qualities. Even the natural qualities are not self-produced but God-given, and therefore reach their highest effectiveness when employed in the service of God and for His glory. . . . The spiritual leader, however, influences others not by the power of his own personality alone but by that personality irradiated and interpenetrated and empowered by the Holy Spirit. Because he permits the Holy Spirit undisputed control of his life, the Spirit's power can flow through him to others uninhibited. Spiritual leadership is a matter of superior power, and that can never be self-generated. There is no such thing as a self-made spiritual leader. (*Spiritual Leadership,* pp. 19-20)

Maintaining balance in spiritual leadership is as challenging as walking a tightrope. We must learn when to flow with His sovereignty and when to press in using the violence of faith to claim His promises. We learn how to be "workers together with Christ" through years of experience. No one but the Great Shepherd can train the inner life of the pastor-shepherd.

All Leaders Face Similar Temptations

The leader is a group's most important member. At times the survival of the group is completely dependent upon his skill and wisdom.

Leaders in any group emerge because they can see a more distant vision than the other members of the community, and they can see how to get the group to that goal. Leaders not only have imagination to improve upon the present, but insight to prepare for the future. They can articulate their program so that others will want to follow.

When you see a flock of geese in the autumn sky heading south for the winter, there is one lead bird at the head of the figure "V" and the other all fall into rank on either side of him, following each in order. In the church we often remark that a man's gift will make room for him. The emergence of a single leader is apparently a law of the universe. God chooses leaders who, in turn, express His wishes directly to the people. And the people can look to their leader as an embodiment and expression of God's will. Asaph said it, "Thou leddest thy people like a flock by the hand of Moses and Aaron" (Psa. 77:20).

To be sure, there are always lesser leaders who come to serve as right-hand men for the chief—whether he is the king, the priest, the military captain, or the pastor-shepherd. But even these close subordinates insist upon a final and ultimate voice of authority. It is instinctive to demand a single visible leader.

The innate self-assertiveness which makes an individual a leader carries with it a special vulnerability to temptations along the line of self-seeking and self-importance. These temptations are shared by all leaders. Few indeed are the persons who have served long in leadership who have successfully avoided all of these snares.

Israel's leaders, though subject to God in a theocratic form of government, failed to remain links between God and the people. They instead set themselves up as the final authority, thereby usurping the place of God in the hearts of the people. No wonder that God thundered warning after warning through the flaming words of His prophets! Here are two scorching examples:

> Then this message came to me from the Lord: Son of dust, prophesy against the shepherds, the leaders of Israel, and say to them: The Lord God says to you: Woe to the

> shepherds who feed themselves instead of their flocks. Shouldn't shepherds feed the sheep? You eat the best food and wear the finest clothes, but you let the flocks starve. You haven't taken care of the weak nor tended the sick nor bound up the broken bones nor gone looking for those who have wandered away and are lost. Instead you have ruled them with force and cruelty. So they were scattered, without a shepherd. They have become a prey to every animal that comes along. (Ezek. 34:1-5 TLB)

> I will send disaster upon the leaders of my people—the shepherds of my sheep—for they have destroyed and scattered the very ones they were to care for. Instead of leading my flock to safety, you have deserted them and driven them to destruction. (Jer. 23:1-TLB)

Ezekiel indicted the shepherds of Israel for three basic leadership sins: exploitation, neglect, and coercive domination. Jeremiah described the result of such abuse as destructive. Not only were the flocks scattered abroad, but the individual sheep were destroyed. The sheep have recourse only to God when a shepherd begins to use them for his own ends, and refuses to heed their objections.

I remember well a growing and flourishing church in one of our southern cities. The pastor-shepherd had an outstanding charisma to lead people. But he believed that he could do no wrong. He was sure God would bless his every move. He threw money around as if it were going out of style.

He exploited his people. He asked them for money to be used in one project or another, but this money never reached its destination. Instead, it lined his own pocket. He borrowed money from members of the congregation and neglected to return it. When he was asked for the repayment of a loan, he swelled with indignation. After all, he was God's man.

I watched the Lord blow upon that church and scatter the sheep in a hundred directions. God will not allow leaders to exploit His sheep.

Another man with outstanding gifts of ministry was suddenly "discovered" and invited to be a speaker in many large and impressive meetings. The spotlight warmed him and he preened like a debutante. But each time he returned home to his local church there was a letdown. His local congregation didn't appreciate him the way his out-of-town audiences did. Consequently, he accepted more and more outside speaking dates. Pride was leading him to a serious neglect of his own sheep—a neglect God will not tolerate in His pastor-shepherds.

Finally, with each return home, this man ran into a kind of civil war. It was only a matter of time until the Lord replaced him and, once he left the place of his pastoral calling, the outside invitations stopped. His neglect of his own sheep at home had tarnished his charisma.

One other instance of charismatic egoism comes to mind. A man of considerable renown was instrumental in opening great avenues of revelation to a number of ministers. In his meetings, he taught the word of God with considerable power. He generally concluded his meetings by laying hands on other clergymen and giving them some word of direction in the name of the Lord. He was so effective in this kind of thing that he began to take himself too seriously.

This came out one time when he wrote a letter to a fellow-pastor of mine who, he felt, was not following the direction he had given him. He said, "As of this date, I am lifting your anointing from your life, and you will begin to recognize your ineffectiveness in only a matter of days." This minister's "star" is presently in eclipse, while the one he threatened continues to pastor a growing flock.

God Protects His Sheep

Sheep are, humanly speaking, helpless against corrupt

shepherds. But God will intervene on their behalf.

> And now I will pour out judgment upon you for the evil you have done to them. And I will gather together the remnant of my flock from wherever I have sent them, and bring them back into their own fold. (Jer. 23:2-3 TLB)

> Therefore, O shepherds, hear the word of the Lord: As I live, says the Lord God, you abandoned my flock, leaving them to be attacked and destroyed, and you were no real shepherds at all, for you didn't search for them. You fed yourselves and let them starve; therefore I am against the shepherds, and I will hold them responsible for what has happened to my flock. I will take away their right to feed the flock—and take away their right to eat. I will save my flock from being taken for food. (Ezek. 34:7-10 TLB)

The expression, "as I live, says the Lord God," is a covenant oath. God will surely bring the shepherds to judgment for every act of evil they have done. He will take away the charisma that has drawn people to them. The sheep will scatter and find better pasture. The shepherds had abandoned the sheep—the effect of God's judgment will be that the sheep will abandon the shepherds. God alone can sever this beautiful relationship. He creates and destroys, and restores.

And we see this judgment happening before our eyes. God is regathering His sheep and restoring genuine pastoral charisma. Ezekiel and Jeremiah not only prophesied the punishment of the shepherds, but the healing and regathering of the sheep.

> For the Lord God says: I will search and find my sheep. I will be like a shepherd looking for his flock. I will find my sheep and rescue them from all the places they were scattered in that dark and cloudy day. And I will bring them back from among the people and nations where they were, back home to their own land of Israel, and I

> will feed them upon the mountains of Israel and by the rivers where the land is fertile and good. Yes, I will give them good pasture on the high hills of Israel. There they will lie down in peace and feed in luscious mountain pastures. I myself will be the Shepherd of my sheep, and cause them to lie down in peace, the Lord God says. I will seek my lost ones, those who strayed away, and bring them safely home again. I will put splints and bandages upon their broken limbs and heal the sick. And I will destroy the powerful, fat shepherds; I will feed them, yes—feed them punishment! (Ezek. 34:11-16 TLB)

We can see God doing all of these things today. In fact, we can list the basic elements of the charismatic renewal and find each of these mentioned in the above prophecy:

(1) God is regathering His people on the basis of spiritual identity—disregarding man-made labels and barriers.
(2) People are rediscovering the Bible as a source of living words—genuine spiritual food.
(3) The rivers are full of the Spirit these days—flowing in worship, in joy, and in fresh revelation from the Lord.
(4) The emphasis upon worship and praise lifts the people into higher levels of receptivity—the good pasture is found on the high hills of awareness that God is present.
(5) The sheep are content and free from alarm, and able to lie down and digest solid teaching.
(6) The Lord is restoring leadership gifts to make His kingdom more apparent—He is actively shepherding His people through His undershepherds.
(7) The church has rediscovered God's healing love; health is being brought to the physically and emotionally ill as well as to the dis-spirited.
(8) No one leader stands out as dominant above all others; God is raising up gifted leadership all over the world, and these

> leaders are learning the necessity of cooperation and fellowship.

Jeremiah's emphasis, as he describes the restoration of God's people, is upon the role of the pastor-shepherd. Centuries ago, he could foresee the restoration of this ministry to its charismatic function and position of respect. He said:

> And I will appoint responsible shepherds to care for them, and they shall not need to be afraid again; all of them shall be accounted for continually. (23:4 TLB)

CHAPTER 24

How Sheep Become Shepherds

I am not only a pastor-shepherd, but also a sheep. I'm not a half-breed either. In the beginning of this book I described a dog in New Zealand who maneuvered an entire flock by nipping at the heels of certain lead sheep. A few sheep in every flock are leaders. They are the key to controlling the entire flock.

A few years ago Pastor Kearney from Australia came to visit us. He taught us a great deal about different kinds of sheep. Among other things, he discussed the butting order and described in considerable detail which kinds of sheep are unqualified to serve as lead sheep.

As the shepherd leads his sheep, there is always one sheep immediately behind him, and after this one, a second and a third. These same lead sheep follow in this order each time the shepherd moves the flock. It is important that the shepherd know these sheep well and understand any idiosyncracies or preferences they might have.

Three kinds of sheep are automatically disqualified from becoming lead sheep because they possess the wrong qualities. They are the hermit sheep, the fence sheep, and the maverick sheep. For the flock to graze and to rest sufficiently, it must be free from tension and alarm. These three kinds of sheep each have a way of introducing discord and anxiety into the sheepfold.

The Hermit Sheep

Hermit sheep refuse to blend with the others, and will not adjust to the rules of the sheepfold. When all other sheep are grazing, the hermit sheep is running around. When the others are lying down, he is off doing his thing.

In the local church, the hermit sheep are the loners. They do not follow their shepherd, but are dominated by inner motivations all their own. The hermit sheep is a free spirit who will not submit to discipline. He makes the entire flock uneasy and tense.

Such a one oftentimes looks as if he possesses great leadership potential because he is self-assertive and goal-directed. He is sure of himself and not easily swayed by the opinions or actions of others. But the other sheep simply will not follow him. They are instinctively suspicious of his leadership because he never cooperates with the shepherd. He is always picking and finding fault, and never leading in constructive ways. His goals are for the betterment of himself rather than the welfare of the flock.

The Fence Sheep

The fence sheep gets his name from his habit of staying so close to the edge that he frequently finds a way to slip out from under the fence. His favorite grazing spots are along the fence rather than in the open field where the other sheep are enjoying good food.

The fence sheep looks away from his own pasture through the fence to the world outside. Since his focus is on what is out of reach, he is always discontent. In his frustration, he often digs holes under the fence to gain freedom to be on his own.

Fence sheep are far too aloof to be involved with the concerns of the flock or the goals of the shepherd. They rarely are informed or up-to-date. Social psychologists call these people marginal because when graphs are drawn to depict social interactions, these people are found to be completely unrelated to the others in a group. Usually such individuals are emotionally unstable and deeply insecure. Their ability to trust in the care of a shepherd has been seriously impaired; they remain apart from others to avoid getting hurt.

Fence sheep pose a serious problem in the management of the sheepfold. Not only do they find holes in the fence and break free, but their lambs follow them. And other sheep near them see them slipping out and are tempted to find out what they are missing on the other side of the fence.

In terms of the local church, the fence sheep are the ones who are nibbling first here and then there. Whenever a new speaker comes to town, they attend the meeting. They follow several radio speakers, subscribe to a number of religious magazines, and support any number of projects around the country. But they cannot be counted on to support the local church's elementary school, to do their share in the nursery, or pay their tithes there. Each new interest eventually loses its charm as they discover that their discontent follows them wherever they go.

They may come back to the local church periodically, but soon they are off again. They are often exploited by traveling ministers who prey upon those who love the spectacular, but they never seem to learn their lesson. After they regain some resources following their most recent fleecing, they are ready to invest again in some other unknown quantity.

The Maverick Sheep

The maverick sheep refuses to be owned by anyone. He always takes an independent course. Webster gives five definitions of a maverick:

(1) An unbranded range animal who is neither a member of a flock nor following its mother.

(2) An individual who bolts at will and sets an independent course.

(3) A person who refuses to conform and takes an unorthodox stand.
(4) One who obtains things by dishonest or questionable means.
(5) A recalcitrant stray.

The maverick is usually a strong person with unusual aggressiveness and determination. But his fatal flaw is his inability to submit to authority. It is impossible to be a genuine leader until one has first become a real follower. The leader himself must be under orders. The maverick is afraid to allow his gifts and talents to be harnessed by the pastor-shepherd. For this reason, no matter how great his abilities may be, he is completely unusable. A person's will must be pliable and he must become a part of the group before he attracts others to follow his leadership.

Maverick sheep sometimes seek to remove a small group from the flock to lead on their own deviant course. But they never seek leadership by lawful means. Instead, they attempt to band dicontented sheep together to attack the leader. For obvious reasons, maverick sheep are a real threat to the peace and well-being of the flock.

Actually, hermit, fence, and maverick sheep are not only unsuited for leadership, often they must be removed from the flock altogether. As long as there is an undercurrent of rebellion within the flock, the sheep remain restless. Action against unruly members is mandatory. Nor is such discipline the idea of pastor-shepherds who dislike having their authority challenged. Whatever real authority they possess has been given to them by God and He is responsible to protect it. Hear the words of the prophet Ezekiel:

> And as for you, O my flock, thus saith the Lord GOD; Behold, I judge between cattle and cattle, between the

> rams and the he goats. Seemeth it a small thing unto you to have eaten up the good pasture, but ye must tread down with your feet the residue of your pastures? and to have drunk of the deep waters, but ye must foul the residue with your feet? And as for my flock, they eat that which ye have trodden with your feet; and they drink that which ye have fouled [or polluted] with your feet. Therefore thus saith the Lord GOD unto them; Behold, I, even I, will judge between the fat cattle and between the lean cattle. Because ye have thrust with side and with shoulder, and pushed all the diseased with your horns, till ye have scattered them abroad; Therefore will I save my flock, and they shall no more be a prey; and I will judge between cattle and cattle. (34:17-22)

The Hebrew word translated "cattle" in this passage denotes small cattle, in other words, lambs and kids, sheep and goats. The Lord is dealing with several forms of selfishness here: competitiveness, covetousness, and cruelty. Such things not only disqualify a person from leadership, but also make him a candidate for discipline and chastening.

How Leaders Emerge

A pastor-shepherd should learn to spot those who have the charisma of the Holy Spirit upon their lives. His task, really, is not to pick but only to confirm what God has already done. That's what the apostles did when the first deacons were chosen. They simply said, "Brethren, look ye out among you seven men of honest report, full of the Holy Ghost and wisdom, whom we may appoint over this business" (Acts 6:3).

The congregation quickly recognized that Stephen, Philip, Prochorus, and others had already demonstrated evident leadership qualities. They had the well-being of the flock uppermost in their mind. When the apostles appointed them to take care of the widows and to make sure the Greek widows got equal treatment with the Jewish widows, they did not regard it as demeaning or beneath their dignity.

I have watched lead sheep emerge from the congregation time and again. These are the ones who delight in serving the flock, who love sharing the word with others, and have an ability to grasp what is going on. Leaders are not born, but rather developed by the groups of which they are a part. These individuals emerge as leaders because they understand more of what is going on than the others.

Philip had a tremendous ability to convey truth, not only to the church members in Jerusalem, but also to their religious enemies in Samaria. Stephen, likewise, was a man of understanding and wisdom.

I like the relationship the apostles had with Philip. He was a bright man who knew his limitations. He realized he was not yet qualified to lay his hands on the Samaritans to receive the Holy Ghost and called for the apostles to do it. Philip recognized that he was teamed with the apostles and was not a "one-man band."

In the Book of Acts we see that the Holy Spirit developed His gifts of leadership within men so that in time they became obvious to everyone. When a person was elevated to a realm of leadership, everyone said amen. God's activity is always supernatural, but seldom is it a flash of lightning bringing change to the social order. It is more often a gradual transition from one level to another until the purposes of God are realized, in a way that seems natural and effortless.

CHAPTER 25

Are All Elders Pastor-Shepherds?

An elder is a mature Christian. He has developed a balanced life, poise of personality, dignity of bearing, and excellence of ministry. He has learned the measure of his faith and how to function within it, not reaching for things beyond his capabilities. Paul described this process of development in these terms:

> For I say, through the grace given unto me, to every man that is among you, not to think of himself more highly than he ought to think; but to think soberly, according as God hath dealt to every man the measure of faith. For as we have many members in one body, and all members have not the same office: So we, being many, are one body in Christ, and every one members one of another. Having then gifts differing according to the grace that is given to us, whether prophecy, let us prophesy according to the proportion of faith; or ministry, let us wait on our ministering: or he that teacheth, on teaching; or he that exhorteth, on exhortation: he that giveth, let him do it with simplicity; he that ruleth, with diligence; he that sheweth mercy, with cheerfulness. (Rom. 12:3-8)

Personal and ministerial development go hand-in-hand. Christ not only makes us whole persons for our own good, but for the good of the whole church. Everybody loves a baby, but no one likes a big baby. People come to maturity when they learn to please God and not themselves.

Maturation does not suddenly give us talents and traits that we did not possess all along. Maturity is the fruition of our God-given potential. Let's allow Webster to refresh our memories:

(1) Maturity is the attainment of the normal peak of growth and development.
(2) Maturity is the reaching of a final or desired state, usually after a period of ripening or processing.
(3) Maturity is the expression of mental and emotional qualities that are considered normal to a socially adjusted adult.
(4) Maturity is ripeness or fitness of time.

In the Epistle to the Ephesians, the apostle speaks of "the measure of the stature of the fulness of Christ." Stature means height. My height is six-foot three inches. That has been my stature since I was seventeen. At that age was I the mature man I am presently? Far from it! I was a tall, dumb kid.

In the Epistle to the Colossians, the apostle adds another dimension which is "knowledge":

> And have put on the new man, which is renewed in knowledge after the image of him that created him. (3:10)

There is much to learn once we have reached full height. To be a skillful person we need to learn how to use our hands, legs, brains, emotions.

When you take your automobile into the service station for repair, you expect someone who is skillful to do the work. If the mechanic heads for your car with a crosscut saw, throw your car into reverse and get out of there fast. A mature mechanic knows his business, his tools, and how to use them. This is true of every mature person, Christian or non-Christian.

Paul defines maturity, in his letter to the Philippians, as full obedience. Christ became obedient unto death, even death on a cross. The shame and suffering of the cross was necessary preparation before Jesus sat down at the right hand of God. Each of us must likewise face the unpleasant realities in life without griping and moaning.

Our prisons teem with men and women who have reached their full height, have skills and talents developed through the years, but it is all for nought because they refused to obey the law. Maturity can be measured in terms of obedience. The childish and immature erroneously think they can disobey and get away with it.

Maturity, then, is the realization of potential. One does not become something brand new, but discovers what God intended him to be from the beginning. God has designed each of us to be unique. Babies look much alike, but when they mature, differences stand out in all their glory—whether naturally or spiritually.

The more we examine the intricacies of nature or read the Scriptures, the more we see God's delight in diversity. Take, for example, the spiritual gifts or manifestations listed by the Apostle Paul:

> Now there are diversities of gifts, but the same Spirit. And there are differences of administrations, but the same Lord. And there are diversities of operations, but it is the same God which worketh all in all. But the manifestation of the Spirit is given to every man to profit withal. For to one is given by the Spirit the word of wisdom; to another the word of knowledge by the same Spirit; To another faith by the same Spirit; to another the gifts of healing by the same Spirit; To another the working of miracles; to another prophecy; to another

> discerning of spirits; to another divers kinds of tongues; to another the interpretation of tongues: But all these worketh that one and the selfsame Spirit, dividing to every man severally as he will. (1 Cor. 12:4-11)

God intends mature believers to experience unity of the Spirit but also to function according to diversity of gift. Each elder is a gifted person according to God's predestinated deposit and years of discipline to develop himself.

Confusion Through the Multiplicity of Words

One common source of confusion about biblical truth is the use of two or more terms to describe the same thing. It sometimes takes time and effort to sort out which words really express differences and which words are, for all practical purposes, synonyms. One such controversy concerns the baptism in the Holy Spirit. This is described by several phrases in the Bible, but the choice of differing terms or phrases does not introduce new doctrinal significance. They are simply several ways of expressing the same concept of God's immersing and inundating a believer in His own presence. Among the more common expressions we find: "the gift of the Spirit," "filled with the Spirit," "the Spirit fell on them," and "baptism in the Spirit."

We face a similar situation when we look at the Greek words for elder: *presbuteros* and *episkopos*. In the English New Testament the former is commonly rendered "elder" and the latter "bishop." But they are really synonymous.

How do we know these words mean the same thing?

First, we do not find these two terms used to designate distinct entities in the New Testament. Bishops and deacons are contrasted (Phil. 1:1; 1 Tim. 3:1, 8), but never bishops and elders. On the other hand we do find at least one instance in which bishops (*episkopoi*) and elders (*presbuteroi*) are used synonymously. "I left you in Crete, that you might . . . appoint elders (*presbuterous*) . . . as I directed you, if any man is blameless, the husband of one wife, and his children are believers and not open to the charge of being profligate or insubordinate. For a bishop (*episkopon*) as God's steward, must be blameless . . ." (Titus 1:5-7, RSV).

The term *presbuteros* was borrowed from the Jewish synagogue with its superintending elders (Luke 7:3). The term *episkopos* was introduced through the Hellenists, for it was a term used in Greek city-states. Both terms in their own context conveyed the idea of superintendence.

But soon after the New Testament was written, people became confused about their meaning. They began to make the *episkopos* superior to *presbuteros*. The Epistles of Ignatius, written early in the second century, already speak of the *episkopos* as not only distinct from but superior to the *presbuteroi*. However, Clement of Rome, who also wrote during the first century, still used the terms synonymously.

Episkopos gradually became a term to distinguish the presiding elder from all other elders or *presbuteroi*. Historians describe this ascendancy of the one-man rulership as the development of episcopacy. As the power of these bishops grew they also began to be regarded as the inheritors of the authority initially invested in the twelve apostles to the Lamb. As this historical process continued, and for a variety of economic and political reasons, the bishop of Rome began to exercise authority over the churches of western Europe, while the patriarch of Constantinople held sway over the eastern churches.

Historians disagree as to exactly how all of this happened. But there are two basic schools of thought. Theodoret and his followers inform us that the episcopate was formed from the apostolic order by localization. The apostles stopped traveling around and settled down to rule in one place.

On the other hand, Lightfoot claimed that the episcopate was formed from the presbyterial order by elevation. Gradually one elder was singled out in a local church to act as an executive.

Whatever the process, the rise of the episcopacy was not warranted by Scripture. Instead, it was born of tendencies within us to construct a hierarchy. Men allowed their own ideas to supercede biblical example and revelation. Frederick W. Dillistone says of this tendency:

> In all the great settled civilisations of the past the *hierarchical* principle has found expression. Up to a point it is imposing and effective. The pyramidal form is one of the most stable known to men. The danger which always arises ultimately, however, is that of the gap—the gap which separates the figures at the highest level of the hierarchy from those at the lowest level. It is all too easy for those at the top to lose vital touch with those of the lower levels, to rely inordinately on the support of those immediately beneath them, to exaggerate their own importance as occupying the position in the hierarchy nearest to the heavenly ideal, to come ultimately to believe that they belong to an entirely different order from that of ordinary human beings and are therefore worthy of a semi-divine status within the community life. Usually this process does not take place consciously or by deliberate design. Once begun, the upward movement towards ever higher hierarchical forms tends to continue until it finally comes to rest in the one who is the last link between earth and heaven. (*Christianity and Symbolism*, p. 123)

What, of course, I want to affirm is that each local church should be a completely autonomous unit, not subject to the supervision of any human agency, be it episcopal or presbyterian. Only the Holy Spirit can sustain the churches in the life of Jesus. And what each congregation needs from Him is a pastor-shepherd genuinely anointed with pastoral charisma.

Paul's departure from Ephesus (Acts 20) was tearful and solemn because, I believe, the apostle was aware that the Holy Spirit had not yet raised up such an anointed pastor for the Ephesians. His farewell was given to the elders of the church, none of whom apparently stood out as peculiarly the leader. It was indeed an occasion for tears as Paul prophesied that "after my departing shall grievous wolves enter in among you, not sparing the flock. Also of your own selves shall men arise, speaking perverse things, to draw away disciples after them" (Acts 20:29-30).

Paul could not designate a pastor-shepherd from among the elders of the Ephesian church, and so the pecking order would follow his departure. The pastoral gift was lacking in this presbytery. They probably had many good gifts and ministries in this leadership group; but not the pastoral charisma.

A pastor-shepherd must be an elder, but this does not automatically mean that each elder is a pastor-shepherd. One elder might have the gift of healing, or the word of wisdom, or the word of knowledge, or the discerning of spirits, or he might be a teacher. The pastoral charisma is a distinct gift and ability given to some persons by the risen Christ.

But it is a common practice in some churches to regard every elder as a pastor-shepherd. These churches have divided into "discipleship cells" with one elder per group as its shepherd. This would hardly be in tune with what we find in the Book of Acts and in the epistles.

When the church at Jerusalem gathered for the first ecumenical council (Acts 15), Luke names three distinct groups: the church, and the apostles and the elders (v. 4).

At this point, the apostles had been the pastor-shepherds or overseers. They were the ones who had established doctrine, lines of fellowship, and guidelines for worship. Through the ensuing years, one man who was not of the original twelve, James, the

Lord's brother, came to be recognized as the pastor-shepherd in Jerusalem. It was James who concluded that momentous council with these words: "Wherefore my sentence is, that we trouble not them, which from among the Gentiles are turned to God" (Acts 15:19). Those are words anointed with God's authority. In the years following, the leadership of the Jerusalem church and the name of James became synonymous. James was considered the pastor-shepherd and there was never a suggestion that the Jerusalem church was divided geographically and each Jerusalem elder shepherded a cell.

CHAPTER 26

Able Ministers of the New Covenant

There is an important difference between the leadership in the Old Testament and in the New. This difference is due to the change God has made in the hearts of those who have entered into the new covenant in Christ. The new covenant is written in hearts of flesh by the inner working of the Holy Spirit, while the old covenant was written in tables of stone and thundered from outside. Thus God's leaders under the old covenant were limited to external means for bringing the sheep into line with God's will. But under the new covenant, the same Holy Spirit who directs the undershepherds is already working deep inside the sheep causing them to will and to do of God's good pleasure (Phil. 2:12-13).

Covenant and commitment are two biblical concepts among many being restored by the Holy Spirit in our time. But we must be careful to use biblical language in the same way the Bible uses it. We are not at liberty to redefine terms to fit modern situations.

Covenant is first of all a contract between God and man. To be sure, there are many examples of inter-human covenants such as that between David and Jonathan. But the everlasting covenant by which the Great Shepherd perfects His sheep speaks of what goes on between God and men (Isa. 42:6; 49:8-10).

If we look at the everlasting covenant as a great river flowing through Scripture, we can then trace many tributaries which have fed into it at various points. Among them are:

(1) the Adamic covenant (Gen. 3:14-17);
(2) the Noahic covenant (Gen. 8:20-9:29);
(3) the Abrahamic covenant (with circumcision) (Gen. 12:1-3; 15; 17; 22:15-18);
(4) the healing covenant (Exod. 15:26; 23:25; Isa. 53);
(5) the Mosaic covenant (Exod. 19, 20, etc.);
(6) the Davidic covenant (2 Sam. 7:1-17; 1 Chron. 17:7-15);
(7) the new covenant (Heb. 8:6-13; 10:1-25; Col. 2:9-13, etc.).

The old covenant includes all the agreements God made with man which led up to the coming of Christ to become sin for us to reconcile us to God. The new covenant is the result of Christ's death, burial, and resurrection, making it possible for the Holy Spirit to live within us and change our hearts. The stony heart of rebellion and resistance is removed and God can write His laws within the heart and mind of the believer—making God's will an inner delight. The new covenant joins the believers to God until they are one spirit (1 Cor. 6:17).

So covenant focuses essentially upon man's relationship with God. Our fellowship with each other is a by-product of redemption. Membership in a local flock comes about because we first belong to the Great Shepherd.

Covenant does not begin with a commitment to men, but to God in Christ. As a result, we are given leaders to perfect us. But these leaders care for us as stewards of Christ's flock, knowing they will one day give account for each sheep.

What About "Coverings"?

God's appointed leaders can never take God's place. Linus, like most of us, is never happy unless his security blanket is nearby. So I'm not surprised to hear a good deal of talk about "covering" in the church today. Most of it says that a man under authority is covered or protected by the one to whom he submits. Thus many ministers are covenanting with one or another leader to be their covering.

But I find no precedent for such a practice in the New Testament. Paul, for example, never covered Peter, nor did Peter cover John. They were vibrant men who fearlessly declared the gospel to the hostile heathen world. What kind of umbrella kept them from succumbing to the pressures which the world system exerted upon them? Did they face the winds of adversity unsheltered?

Throughout the New Testament we find the significant phrase "in Christ" which makes all the difference. Until a person has come "into Christ," he is still limited to the natural. But once he comes in through the Door of Jesus Christ and is placed in the body, the Bible calls him a literal "new creation." Listen to the Apostle Paul:

> Wherefore henceforth know we no man after the flesh: yea, though we have known Christ after the flesh, yet now henceforth know we him no more. Therefore if any man be in Christ, he is a new creature: old things are passed away; behold, all things are become new. And all things are of God, who hath reconciled us to himself by Jesus Christ, and hath given to us the ministry of reconciliation. (2 Cor. 5:16-18)

Coming into Christ is far more important than most church people realize; it is the difference between life and death. We become new people when we are joined to Christ by a new birth and bound up in Him in terms of the new covenant. Before this time, we were dead, naked, and undone by sin and our rebellious nature. But "in Christ" we are made alive. We are clothed with His own righteousness and made partakers of His nature. Paul tells us that as part of our conversion-initiation experience of entering in at the door, we receive our covering. Listen to his words to the Galatians:

> For as many of you as have been baptized into Christ have put on Christ. There is neither Jew nor Greek, there is neither bond nor free, there is neither male nor female: for ye are all one in Christ Jesus. And if ye be Christ's, then are ye Abraham's seed, and heirs according to the promise. (3:27-29)

It is significant that these words are so clearly expressed in the epistle of liberty. The Galatian church had been facing problems because they misunderstood the relationship of the old and new Covenants. They were still working under the assumption that God deals from the outside, whereas in Christ He works from the inside out. Paul was required to clarify the fact that all other covenants had been fulfilled in the person of Christ. In Him we are heirs to all the covenants and promises of God.

Those who insist upon a man-made covering fail to understand the inheritance we have already received in Christ—a covering so complete that it is inconceivable that it could be supplemented. One way that Christ protects us is by destroying the former distinctions made by God through the Sinaitic covenant, for Paul informed the Ephesians:

> But now in Christ Jesus ye who sometimes were far off are made nigh by the blood of Christ. For he is our peace, who hath made both one, and hath broken down the middle wall of partition between us; Having abolished in his flesh the enmity, even the law of commandments contained in ordinances; for to make in himself of twain one new man, so making peace. (2:13-15)

When we visited the Holy Land I saw this wall of partition separating not only the Jew from the Gentile, but men from women. What a pitiful sight it was! This experience made a vivid impression on me and I understood the importance of Paul's words all the more. Christ is a great leveler. No matter what we were before coming into Him, we are made one in Him.

There at the wailing wall I was given a yarmulke or little cap to place on the back of my head. I was not allowed to approach this most holy place without my head covered. After I had been to the wall, I drew back and viewed the scene from a distance. On the right side of the wall of partition the women approached the holy wall, veiled and covered. I knew then that Christ had brought a tremendous liberty to all mankind—men and women—when He opened up a new and living way into the presence of God.

A woman has the right to approach God on her own without asking permission from anyone, her husband and local elder included. I take my thoughts, ambitions, and desires to the Lord without gaining clearance from any man. I can talk to Him about the automobile I want to buy, or the house, or the suit of clothes, or anything. To seek permission from someone who is providing me with a so-called covering is ludicrous. Whom the Son sets free is free indeed!

Covenant Love

The two different terms for "love" in the Old Testament have been distinguished as election-love versus covenant-love. Election-love is close to our New Testament concept of grace. It arises freely from God and is totally unmerited.

Covenant-love, on the other hand, refers to faithfulness once a person or nation has been joined to God by covenant. Covenant-love is expressed in terms of duty and loyalty.

When God shows covenant-love to His people, He demonstrates loyalty and faithfulness to carry out His promises. Those bound in covenant were expected to respond to God by giving Him loyal service and obedience. God would give kindness and help, and He would even give punishment if this would restore a disrupted covenant relationship. In other words, God's anger, jealousy, and discipline are a part of His faithfulness in covenant-love.

To summarize: election-love stimulates God to unconditionally select a people for himself; covenant-love is both God's faithfulness to fulfill all the love He has pledged, and man's response of loyal devotion to God.

Because words like faithfulness, loyalty, fidelity, devotion, etc., no longer grip our imaginations as they once did, some Christian teachers have sought to use the term "covenant-love" to express the idea of commitment to one another and its attendant obligations of mutual loyalty.

We need to renew the concept of commitment, but it's sad that this has become confused with other issues such as cell groups and slavish obedience to some elder who is not a pastor-shepherd of a local church. Throughout the New Testament, man's commitment focused primarily upon the Lord himself, and secondarily toward fellow members of the body of Christ. Loyalty and commitment were expressed in daily life as Christians who loved Jesus ministered one to another. We find nothing in the New Testament to suggest a smaller covenant circle working apart from the entire local assembly.

Why has covenant-love come to our attention in these days? The Holy Spirit is calling our attention to an area of lack. This controversy underscores the need to restore covenant commitment in the context of the average local assembly. God is calling afresh for love toward one another, and especially for a love that is practical in lifting heavy burdens and comforting the needy. The pastor-shepherd and his ministerial associates cannot do it for us. From the beginning, God has expected us all to show care toward one another. Realizing this requires repentance and restoration on the part of all; it does not require a restructuring of the community into small neighborhood groups.

Those under Moses became dependent upon him. They were unable to approach God for themselves. But in contrast, those under the new covenant depend on no man; each experiences God for himself. They are to be led but not coerced, fed but not prohibited from liberty to discover God's word by the help of the Holy Spirit.

Paul strongly opposed false teachers who sought to lord it over the flock. His opponents relied upon man-made credentials and traditions. Paul did not need to defend himself in these terms because his authority was born of the Spirit.

> Are we beginning to be like those false teachers of yours who must tell you all about themselves and bring long letters of recommendation with them? I think you hardly need someone's letter to tell you about us, do you? And we don't need a recommendation from you, either! The only letter I need is you yourselves! By looking at the good change in your hearts, everyone can see that we have done a good work among you. They can see that you are a letter from Christ, written by us. It is not a letter written with pen and ink, but by the Spirit of the living God; not one carved on stone, but in human hearts. (2 Cor. 3:1-3 TLB)

Under the old covenant, people's hearts were as hard against God as the stone tablets on which the Ten Commandments were inscribed. But once the stony heart was replaced by a heart of flesh, as the Holy Spirit took up permanent residence under the new covenant, it became an easier matter to impress God's desires upon men's hearts and minds. Christ could be formed within the believers both through the teaching and examples of their leaders. The good pastor-shepherd according to new covenant standards, is the one who most faithfully imprints the image of the Great Shepherd within the sheep.

Paul was not writing to a half dozen people in some home, but to an established local assembly, probably of several hundred sheep. He had written the message of Christ upon their hearts and minds not by individualized attention but through systematic preaching, setting a good example, and through local church discipline. He had not worked alone but used others with varying ministry gifts to assist in perfecting the sheep. As we study the two Corinthian letters and other New Testament evidence, we would be hard put to find a ministry more effective than Paul's. The able minister of the new covenant clearly functions best within the context of the local church, in an atmosphere of liberty created by the Holy Spirit's activity among the flock.

BIBLIOGRAPHY

Allen, Clifton J., Gen. Ed., *The Broadman Bible Commentary*. Nashville: Broadman Press, 1970.

Bridges, Charles. *The Christian Ministry*. London: Banner of Truth Trust, 1959.

Dillistone, Frederick W. *Christianity and Symbolism*. Philadelphia: Westminster Press, 1903.

Encyclopaedia Britannica, 14th ed., s.v. "Sheep—Care and Management."

Hastings, James. *A Dictionary of the Bible*. New York: Charles Scribner's Sons, 1903.

Krikorian, M.P. *The Spirit of the Shepherd*. Grand Rapids: Zondervan, 1938.

Mackie, G.M. *Bible Manners and Customs*. New York: Fleming H. Revell Co., n.d.

Meyer, F.B. *The Shepherd Psalm*. Fort Washington, Pa.: Christian Literature Crusade, 1953.

Miller, Madeleine S. and J. Lane. *Encyclopedia of Bible Life*. New York: Harper and Row, 1944.

Moghabghab, Faddoul. *The Shepherd Song on the Hills of Lebanon*. New York: E.P. Dutton & Co., 1907

Our Amazing World of Nature: Its Marvels. Pleasantville, New York: Reader's Digest Press, 1969.

Paul, Robert S. *The Church in Search of Itself*. Grand Rapids: William B. Eerdmans Publ. Co., 1972.

Pink, Arthur W. *Exposition of the Gospel of John*. Grand Rapids: Zondervan, 1945.

Robertson, J.A. "The Primitive Ministry." *Essays on the Early History of the Church and the Ministry* Edited by H.B. Swete. London: Macmillan, 1918

Sanders, J. Oswald. *Spiritual Leadership*. Chicago: Moody Bible Institute, 1967.

Spurgeon, Charles H. *Spurgeon's Expository Encyclopedia*. Grand Rapids: Baker Book House, 1951.

Thomson, William M. *The Land and the Book*. Grand Rapids: Baker Book House, 1954.

Wright, Fred. *Manners and Customs of Bible Lands* Chicago: Moody Press, 1953